British
WILDLIFE

British
WILDLIFE

Written by:

Camille de la Bédoyère

Miles
KeLLY

First published in 2008 by
Miles Kelly Publishing Ltd,
Harding's Barn, Bardfield End Green,
Thaxted, Essex, CM6 3PX, UK

Copyright © Miles Kelly Publishing Ltd 2008

This edition printed in 2013

2 4 6 8 10 9 7 5 3 1

Publishing Director Belinda Gallagher

Creative Director Jo Cowan

Editorial Assistant Sarah Parkin

Cover Designer Jo Cowan

Designer Joe Jones

Production Manager Elizabeth Collins

Reprographics Stephan Davis,
Thom Allaway

Archive Manager Jennifer Hunt

ISBN 978-1-78209-127-1

Printed in China

British Library Cataloguing-in-Publication Data
A catalogue record for this book is
available from the British Library

Made with paper from a sustainable forest

www.mileskelly.net
info@mileskelly.net
www.factsforprojects.com

CONTENTS

MAMMALS

BE A WILDLIFE DETECTIVE

The British countryside, woodlands, parks and gardens are home to many different animals. Some of our wildlife is very easy to spot. However, some creatures are harder to find. There are useful pieces of equipment that may help you to find many of the animals listed in this book, and a few handy hints to set you safely on your way.

USEFUL TOOLS FOR DETECTIVE WORK

Binoculars

It is almost impossible to get close enough to birds to get a good look at the shape of their bills or the colour of their legs. A pair of binoculars magnifies things and makes them appear larger, so identification becomes much easier.

Magnifying glass

Many invertebrates, such as ants and bugs, are too small to see clearly with the naked eye. A magnifying glass allows you to see their limbs, antennae and other interesting details.

Notebook and pencil

You can record notes and make sketches in this book. Sketching an animal makes you look closely at its features, which is good for improving your detective skills. Taking photographs is another useful way of keeping records.

Small containers

Old shells, feathers and other interesting specimens can be kept in these and taken home for further examination. Never take anything living home or disturb an animal's habitat.

HANDY HINTS FOR DETECTIVE WORK

When you go out in search of wildlife you should follow these simple rules:

1. Shut gates after you or farm animals may escape and come to harm.
2. Keep dogs under control because they scare other animals away.
3. Stay on or near the paths so you don't stray onto other people's land or get lost.
4. Do not pick plants, but you can collect some leaves.
5. Respect the animals' habitats or homes.

Stay safe If you are exploring a new area take a map with you. It is always a good idea to take food and water. Never venture out without telling an adult where you are going and when you plan to return.

Use your ears Occasionally just stand or sit still and listen. You may be able to hear all sorts of interesting wildlife noises, especially in summer. If you stay in one place for long enough, some animals may come up to investigate you!

Look and look again Most animals are hidden from view, so you will need to peer inside hedgerows, lift up leaves and raise logs and rocks to see what may be lurking underneath. One golden rule is always put things back the way you found them.

Keep quiet Most animals fear being caught, and so they react quickly to the slightest sound. Unless you are looking for wildlife in silence, most of the interesting animals will have disappeared from view long before you get close to them.

BRITISH WILDLIFE

Animals that have lived in Britain for thousands of years are described as being 'native'. Some of our native animals are so common you will probably already be familiar with them.

Blackbird

With their black plumage (feathers) and yellow bills, male blackbirds are easy to identify. However, females are much harder to recognize because they are brown all over, with a speckled breast. Blackbirds hop through leaf litter searching for insects, berries and worms to eat.

▼ *Blackbirds are familiar garden birds, but they can also be spotted in woodland and farmland.*

Woodlouse

These bugs are amongst the easiest to find, especially in woodland and garden habitats. Despite their appearance, these animals are crustaceans, not insects. This means they are more closely related to crabs than they are to beetles!

▼ *Pill woodlice are able to roll into a ball when they are disturbed.*

Mallard

The most common ducks in the world, mallards live not only in Britain but throughout Europe, Asia, Africa and North America. The males, which are called drakes, have bottle-green heads and black, grey and white bodies. In summer, they lose this bright colouring and take on the same dull brown plumage as the females. Mallards are usually tame and approach people for food.

▲ *Mallards are very adaptable and can live in almost all types of aquatic habitats.*

Pony

In some of Britain's wilder places ponies roam free. Dartmoor, Exmoor, Shetland and New Forest ponies are all examples of these stocky and tough animals that can survive in harsh habitats.

▶ *Shetland ponies have long, thick fur and manes to keep them warm and protect them from the cold.*

Wasp

If you spot many wasps in one place it is likely you are near a nest. These stinging insects live in large groups of up to 1000 individuals, and they build their nests in old burrows, garden sheds or house lofts. It is unwise to bother wasps near a nest because they can produce a special smell called a pheromone, which calls other wasps to come to their aid.

▼ *These wasps will not store food in their nest, as the cells face downwards and are open at the bottom.*

Song thrush

These birds look very similar to mistle thrushes (pages 122–123), but they are smaller and have slightly darker colouring. Song thrushes often scuttle across the ground, head leaning over to one side, as they listen for insects. Their songs are loud and sung at dusk.

Woodpigeon

Large, grey, stout-bodied birds, woodpigeons are common in parks, gardens, woodlands and farms. They waddle when they walk and are able to eat all sorts of food. The pigeons that are found in towns are likely to be rock, or feral, pigeons, which are smaller than woodpigeons.

ANIMALS FROM ABROAD

Britain has only been an island for about 8000 years. Before then, animals roamed freely across a large landmass, which included Britain. Since then, British wildlife has been largely cut off from Europe. However, people have introduced new species, or types, of animal to Britain, many of which have settled and established populations. These animals are called non-native species.

Parakeet

Parrots and parakeets mostly live in hot, tropical countries. However, an increasingly large number of these birds are now living wild in Britain, especially in the southeast. The birds were probably pets that escaped or were set free and they have adapted well to the cooler British climate.

▼ *Male and female rose-ringed parakeets differ slightly in appearance – females lack the pink collar and black facial markings.*

Muntjac

Small deer from Asia, muntjacs were brought to Britain about 100 years ago. A number of them escaped from the wildlife park where they lived and successful groups of muntjacs have since grown.

Mink

American minks have escaped from fur farms in Britain and now live wild in the countryside. These mammals threaten vole populations in the areas where they live and are considered pests.

Red-necked wallaby

These animals come from Tasmania, a small island off Australia. They were brought to British zoos but those that escaped have bred in the wild. There are now two small populations in Sussex and the Peak District.

◀ *The red-necked wallaby is one of the largest wallabies, so it can easily be mistaken for a kangaroo.*

Red-eared terrapin

Terrapins are a type of reptile. The red-eared terrapin is an American species that has become widespread in Britain. Originally kept as pets, these animals can grow quite large and give a nasty bite, so many have been released into the wild. Unfortunately, they attack and eat ducklings.

▶ *The red-eared terrapin can easily be identified by the red stripe behind it's ears. It is fond of basking in the sunshine.*

▼ *Squirrels scurry about in trees or on the ground, looking for food such as nuts.*

Grey squirrel

These small mammals were first introduced to Britain from the USA around 100 years ago, and they have settled over large parts of the country. Sadly, grey squirrels have forced the native red squirrel out of most of its natural habitat.

Common pheasant

These long-tailed, brightly coloured birds originally came from Asia, and they have been living in Britain for hundreds of years. They were brought here as game birds, which could be hunted for sport.

▼ *An adult male pheasant is unmistakeable with its green head, red eye patch and long tail.*

IDENTIFYING VERTEBRATES

Scientists sort animals into groups according to their characteristics, such as the number of legs. This helps to identify the animals and work out how they are related to one another. Learning about these groups will help you become a better wildlife detective.

Vertebrates

Animals that have backbones are called vertebrates.

Animals without backbones are called invertebrates.

Vertebrates have brains and complex nervous systems.

The nervous system helps an animal gather information about the world around it and react to that information. A vertebrate has good senses, such as sight and smell. They usually have complex lifestyles and have developed different types of behaviour.

▲ *This tadpole has hatched from an egg and is able to swim. It will grow into an adult frog.*

Amphibians lay their eggs in water and many of them need to live in or near a damp habitat to survive. They have moist skin that can absorb oxygen and in some cases produces toxins, or poisons, to protect the animal from predators. The young often look very different to the adult, for example, tadpoles, which are young frogs.

Reptiles have scaly bodies. Their young hatch from eggs, which are laid on land. They cannot control their temperature as well as mammals can, so they hibernate when it is cold or bask in the sun.

▶ *Green lizards are good climbers and can climb walls, trees and bushes quickly.*

Fish are water-living vertebrates with bodies that are adapted for their habitat. Most fish have torpedo-shaped bodies that can move easily through the water. They breathe using special organs called gills, which absorb oxygen from the water. Most fish have scales on their bodies.

▼ Fallow deer live in wooded areas, as part of a medium-sized herd.

Mammals are vertebrates that have fur, or hair, and they feed their young with milk that is produced by the mother's body. The young are born and not hatched from eggs. Mammals are able to control their body temperature, which means they can survive in cold places. Most mammals have four limbs, although in bats, the forelimbs are wings. The smallest wild British mammals are shrews and bats. Long ago, other mammals, such as bears and wolves, also lived in Britain.

Birds are vertebrates that have feathers and bills (beaks). Their hind limbs are adapted for perching. Their front limbs are wings and most birds can fly. Young birds hatch from eggs.

▶ Robins are highly territorial. They are usually seen alone or in pairs during spring and summer.

IDENTIFYING INVERTEBRATES

More than 90 percent of all living animals are invertebrates – creatures without backbones. This group includes arthropods such as insects, annelids such as worms, and molluscs such as snails.

Arthropods are invertebrates with bodies that are protected by a hard outer skin, or exoskeleton. Their bodies are usually divided into segments. There are four main groups of arthropods:
- Insects
- Crustaceans
- Spiders
- Millipedes and centipedes

Millipedes and centipedes are arthropods that live on land and have many pairs of legs. Each body segment has either one pair of legs (centipedes) or two (millipedes).

▶ *Centipedes catch prey with their claws.*

Insects have bodies that are divided into three segments: the head, the thorax and the abdomen. Three pairs of legs are attached to the thorax, and, if there are any, wings too. The heads have the sensory organs such as eyes and antennae.

▼ *Butterflies, like this small tortoiseshell butterfly, are attracted to gardens because they feed on nectar from buddleia flowers.*

Crustaceans have two pairs of antennae and eyes on stalks. Most crustaceans live in water, but some, such as woodlice, live on land.

▶ *Many spiders spin webs to catch their prey.*

Spiders' bodies have two main segments and four pairs of legs. Spiders often have more than two eyes and can produce silk from their abdomens.

Annelids are worms with bodies that are divided into segments, for example, earthworms. Each segment of a worm's body contains a complete set of organs. Most worms are burrowers.

▶ *Earthworms spend most of their time underground. However, they do come to the surface at night and in wet weather.*

▲ *Snails eat plants using their rough mouthpart, called a radula, which scrapes and grazes food.*

Molluscs include octopuses, squids, garden snails and slugs and shelled sea creatures. These animals have soft bodies and no skeleton. Their soft body may be protected by a hard shell. Molluscs have rough tongues and a 'foot'. This part of their body is used for movement.

WILDLIFE HOTSPOTS

Britain's National Parks are home to some fascinating creatures, including many that you would be unlikely to spot in a garden. There are over 6000 National Parks in the world, covering about 12 percent of the Earth's surface, and 14 of them are in England, Wales and Scotland. Britain's first National Park, the Peak District, was set up in 1951.

New Forest

Rare types of animal found here include the sand lizard, New Forest cicada and the honey buzzard. It is a good place to find lizards and snakes.

▼ Stag beetles are now scarce but can be found in the New Forest National Park.

Brecon Beacons

A mountainous park with spectacular scenery, the Brecon Beacons are a good place to spot lapwings, otters, water voles and great crested newts.

◄ Otters' numbers have been affected in recent years due to hunting, water pollution and the loss of their river habitat. They can be spotted in the Brecon Beacons.

The Broads

A huge area of wetland in this park means it is a good place to spot birds, fish, invertebrates and amphibians that like damp habitats. Frogs, dragonflies, herons, mallards, kingfishers and newts may be seen.

Pembrokeshire Coast

The only entirely coastal national park, the Pembrokeshire Coast is a good place to find water and coastal birds. You can also look out for seals, porpoises, dolphins and even whales or basking sharks.

Cairngorms

Heathlands, woodlands, rivers and lochs provide plenty of interesting habitats in the Cairngorms. Look out for red deer, sika deer, reindeer, red squirrels and birds of prey, especially ospreys and falcons.

▼ *Red squirrels are now common only in northern England and the Scottish Highlands.*

Northumberland

The peaceful hills and valleys of Northumberland are particularly good places to spy insects and birds. Emperor moths, peacock butterflies, martins, swallows and cuckoos are all to be found here.

▼ *Badgers can also be spotted in Northumberland National Park.*

Lake District

Britain's largest national park, the Lake District provides a range of habitats. Look out for red squirrels, golden eagles, ospreys, pipistrelle bats, toads and the high brown fritillary butterfly.

▲ *Swallows are common summer visitors to most of Britain and Ireland.*

Dartmoor

The largest and wildest open space in southern England, Dartmoor is home to a huge variety of wildlife, such as swifts, swallows, field voles, common lizards and hedgehogs.

Peak District

With heather moors, bogs, woodlands, rivers and cliffs, the Peak District has many habitats. Wildlife includes polecats, water shrews and water voles, although voles are becoming increasingly rare.

SPRING AND SUMMER

Spring is the season of new life. Most habitats are buzzing with activity, as plants burst into leaf and provide food for animals that are emerging from their winter hibernations. By early summer, many creatures have produced their young and there is plenty of food available. The warmer weather is kinder to immature creatures that would not survive cold temperatures. These are the best seasons for wildlife watching.

Trees in bloom

In spring, trees produce their blooms, which attract insects. The insects are drawn to the flowers by their bright colours and sweet scents. They suck nectar, which is a sugary solution produced by the plant. As they travel between plants, insects pick up a fine yellow dust called pollen. When this is brushed over the surface of a flower's female parts, it fertilises the eggs. These develop into seeds.

▼ *Some trees burst into blossom in spring. Insects emege from hibernation, or from their eggs or pupae, to drink the nectar.*

◄ *Famous for its musical song, this nightingale can be heard both day and night.*

Songs for spring

Birds usually mate in spring and their courtship often involves singing to attract a mate. Using a pair of binoculars, you may be able to identify the singers. If you encounter a nest do not approach it. You may scare the parent birds who can sometimes abandon nests once they have been disturbed.

Tasty leaves

Many invertebrates are busy munching through large quantities of leaves in the spring. Look out for damaged leaves and flowers and you may be able to spot the creature that is feasting on the plant.

▶ *Snails eat leaves at dusk and leave tell-tale holes and slime trails.*

Snakes and lizards

Summer is the best time to find these shy creatures because they like to sit in the sun, soaking up its heat. Snakes and lizards can move with lightning speed and blend easily into the vegetation. You need to look for them carefully and quietly.

Summer by the sea

Summertime visits to the seaside provide a fantastic opportunity for the wildlife detective. There are rock pools to explore and lots of gulls and wading birds, such as herring gulls, terns and cormorants, to spot. Seals and dolphins may be seen along some coasts and harbours.

▶ *Grey seals come ashore to mate and give birth. They stay mostly in coastal waters and are common off the west coast of Britain and Ireland.*

AUTUMN AND WINTER

In autumn, trees and plants are laden with fruits and seeds, tempting animals to feast on them before the winter sets in. Migrating birds fill the skies, with the summer visitors returning to their warmer homes and birds from colder regions coming to Britain for the winter.

Preparing to hibernate

Many small mammals cannot survive frosts and snowfalls, so they spend the winter tucked away in burrows or beneath piles of vegetation. Before they settle down to hibernate, these animals must eat as much as possible to build up the layers of fat that will help them survive the cold months. Many insects also hibernate.

▲ Autumn is a good time to see a spider's web in full glory. Many creatures, such as flies, get caught in the web.

Owls on the prowl

As leaves fall, bird-spotting becomes much easier. Tawny owls are common in towns as well as the countryside, and their large outlines can be spied at night, perching in the treetops. In the autumn, owls start competing for their territories so they are particularly noisy.

Spiders' webs

In the autumn and winter, dew settles on spiders' webs, highlighting their extraordinary structure. These arthropods are most active at night, along with other invertebrates, such as snails and slugs.

Fighting deer

October sees the annual deer ruts. Males fight one another for the right to mate with the females, and their spectacular displays of antler crashing are fascinating to watch.

◀ These red deer stags are rutting in the snow. They are fighting for the female deer and will make roaring, bellowing sounds.

Winter coats

In northern regions, stoats and hares grow beautiful white coats in the winter. These not only help camouflage the animals against a frosty, snowy landscape, but may also help them to conserve heat.

▶ *This stoat's coat has turned white for winter but the tail tip remains black. The fur is known as ermine.*

Super salmon

In November, salmon embark on their incredible journeys upstream, where they will spawn, or lay their eggs. These journeys take place soon after the first heavy rains, in clear rivers.

Fox calls

In winter, foxes become very active as they search for mates. They bark and scream to draw attention to themselves. Although these animals are nocturnal, they can be seen once the sun begins setting, which occurs in the afternoon at this time of year.

▲ *Foxes are secretive animals but they become very noisy during breeding season in winter.*

HOW TO USE THIS BOOK

Use this guide to help you find your way around this book. There's information about 101 different species of British wildlife, amazing facts and measurements and a photo file. You can add your own notes and pictures in the write-in area.

Photo file
See a close-up of each animal or plant in its natural habitat.

Fact file
Packed with essential facts and information.

Super fact
Find out lots of amazing facts about each species.

Write-in area
Draw pictures and add notes, ideas and thoughts about anything you see.

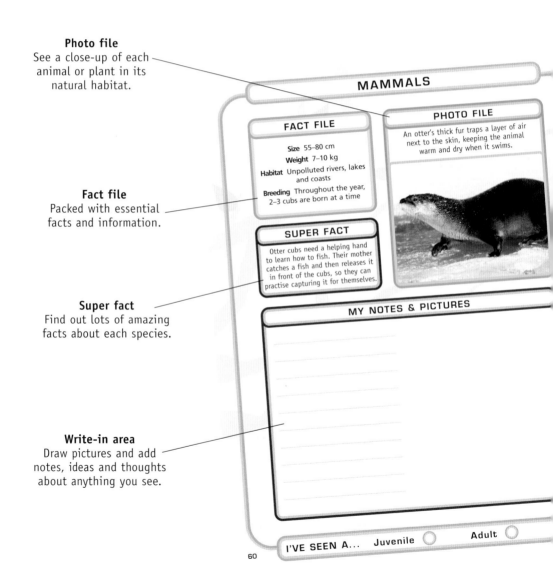

MAMMALS

FACT FILE

Size 55–80 cm
Weight 7–10 kg
Habitat Unpolluted rivers, lakes and coasts
Breeding Throughout the year, 2–3 cubs are born at a time

PHOTO FILE

An otter's thick fur traps a layer of air next to the skin, keeping the animal warm and dry when it swims.

SUPER FACT

Otter cubs need a helping hand to learn how to fish. Their mother catches a fish and then releases it in front of the cubs, so they can practise capturing it for themselves.

MY NOTES & PICTURES

I'VE SEEN A... Juvenile ○   Adult ○

60

SCALE GUIDE

The wildlife in this book is compared against something you are familiar with. This will help you to understand how big or small it actually is. The bugs, however, are shown at actual size.

A cat's body is about 50 cm in length

OTTER *Lutra lutra*

Sighting an otter by a riverbank is a rare treat. These animals are very shy and likely to disappear beneath the water's surface when they are disturbed. They mostly feed on fish, but they will also eat water birds or frogs. Otters find it hard to survive in polluted water and this has affected their numbers in recent years. They have also been hunted for their fur and to stop them eating fish.

SCALE

Main text
Every right-hand page introduces you to each animal.

Smooth, brown fur

Long, slender body

Pale on underside

Short legs

Webbed feet

Thick tail

Illustration
Images have labels to help you identify each species.

Keep a record
Tick the circles to show what you've seen and where you've seen it.

AT THE... River ◯ Lake ◯ Coast ◯   61

FACT FILE

Size 67–90 cm

Weight 8–12 kg

Habitat Woodland, farmland, parks, other open areas

Breeding Most cubs are born January–March

SUPER FACT

Badgers use their strong claws and powerful legs to dig up bee and wasp nests in order to feed on honey and larvae.

PHOTO FILE

Badgers live in communities, or clans, and hide away in their huge networks of burrows and tunnels called setts.

MY NOTES & PICTURES

I'VE SEEN A... Juvenile ◯   Adult ◯

BADGER _Meles meles_

These animals live in the countryside, in woodland and on large commons. Badgers occasionally wander into gardens and farmland, but as they are nocturnal, seeing a badger is rare. If they come close to human homes, they may be searching for food and will scavenge in rubbish bins. Badgers are omnivorous – they eat both meat and plants. Male badgers are called boars, the females are called sows, and their young are known as cubs.

SCALE

Short tail (females have bushier tails than males)

Thick, coarse, slate-grey fur

Small, pointed head and short neck

Short, strong legs with sharp claws for digging

Black stripes mark its white face

IN THE... Garden ◯　　Park ◯　　Countryside ◯

FACT FILE

Size 1.9–4 m

Weight Up to 650 kg

Habitat Ocean, harbours, bays, river mouths

Breeding Calving takes place all year round

SUPER FACT

Bottlenose dolphins live in oceans and seas around the world. Those found around the coast of Britain are amongst the largest and heaviest of all.

PHOTO FILE

Groups of around 20 dolphins can be seen near coasts, but groups of several hundred are found in the deeper ocean.

MY NOTES & PICTURES

I'VE SEEN A... Juvenile ◯ Adult ◯

BOTTLENOSE DOLPHIN

Tursiops truncatus

The sight of a group of bottlenose dolphins leaping out of the water is an unforgettable treat. These mammals are social animals and often appear near the coast in a group, or school. Sometimes it is possible to spy them surfing the waves, jumping several metres out of the water, or even tossing seaweed around in what appears to be a game. Bottlenose dolphins are also known as grey porpoises, black porpoises and cowfish.

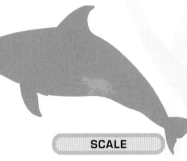

SCALE

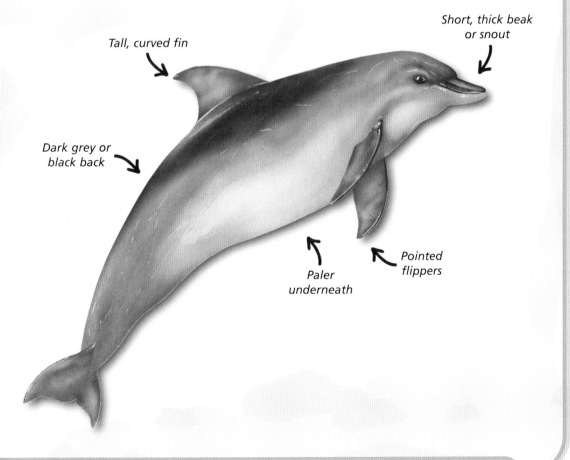

Tall, curved fin

Short, thick beak or snout

Dark grey or black back

Paler underneath

Pointed flippers

MAMMALS

FACT FILE

Size 50–80 cm

Weight 4–7 kg

Habitat Grasslands, farms, hedgerows

Breeding Up to three litters every year, with 1–4 young each time

SUPER FACT

Courtship takes place in spring, giving rise to the phrase 'mad March hare'. Females stand on their hind legs and 'box' one another in a fight over mates!

PHOTO FILE

To avoid being seen by predators, hares keep very still and crouch low. They hold their ears back, listening for any sudden movements.

MY NOTES & PICTURES

I'VE SEEN A... Juvenile ◯ Adult ◯

BROWN HARE *Lepus europaeus*

Very fast runners, brown hares can reach speeds of 60 km/h when trying to escape a predator. Brown hares have orangey-brown fur and long slender ears with black tips. Hares are herbivores (they only eat plants). They are hunted by foxes and young hares may be caught by birds of prey. Hares are often found in open grassland and may wander into nearby gardens, but they are easily scared away.

SCALE

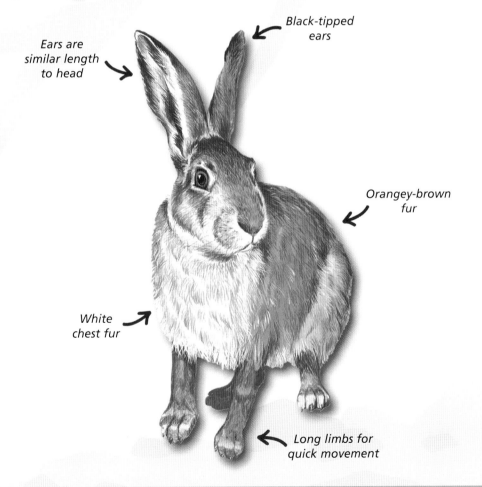

Black-tipped ears

Ears are similar length to head

Orangey-brown fur

White chest fur

Long limbs for quick movement

IN THE... Garden ◯   Park ◯   Countryside ◯

MAMMALS

FACT FILE

Size Wingspan 24–28 cm

Weight 5–15 g

Habitat Woodlands, orchards, parks

Breeding Mate in autumn and produce one young in mid-June

SUPER FACT

Long-eared bats deserve their name because their ears measure three-quarters the length of their bodies. That's like a human having ears that reach to their knees!

PHOTO FILE

Brown long-eared bats hibernate over winter, spending the cold months in tree holes, caves, hollow walls, tunnels and mines.

MY NOTES & PICTURES

I'VE SEEN A... Juvenile Adult ◯

BROWN LONG-EARED BAT *Plecotus auritus*

Like most other bats, brown long-eared bats live on a diet of insects. They come out at night and dart around the skies on the hunt for food. Their hearing is so good that these little mammals can detect a single insect on the ground just by the noise it makes as it walks. Brown long-eared bats are also known as whispering bats because they produce sounds that are extremely quiet.

SCALE

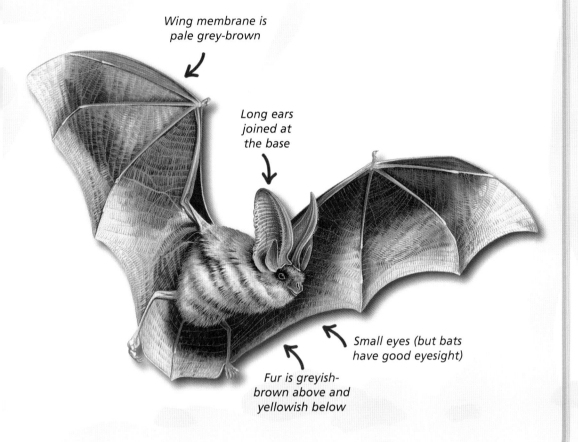

Wing membrane is pale grey-brown

Long ears joined at the base

Small eyes (but bats have good eyesight)

Fur is greyish-brown above and yellowish below

IN THE... Garden ◯   Park ◯   Countryside ◯

MAMMALS

FACT FILE

Size 11–28 cm

Weight 200–400 g

Habitat All habitats, especially farmland

Breeding Breed constantly and females have about five litters a year

SUPER FACT

Compost heaps are a perfect place for rats to breed. The compost keeps them warm and there is a steady supply of food.

PHOTO FILE

Brown rats are rarely seen because they are most active at night. They are omnivores and often steal eggs from other animals.

MY NOTES & PICTURES

I'VE SEEN A... Juvenile ◯ Adult ◯

COMMON RAT *Rattus norvegicus*

Also known as brown rats, these **rodents live almost everywhere that humans live.** They are found in towns, cities and the countryside – anywhere they can find food. They are often associated with dirty places, such as rubbish heaps and sewers, but rats also live in hedgerows and fields. They are highly intelligent creatures with natural curiosity. They can live in large groups, or colonies, and fight one another for the best territory.

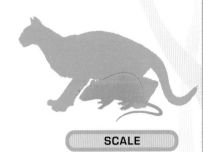

SCALE

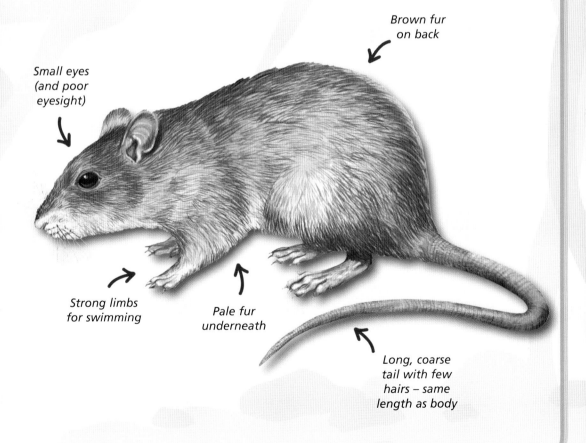

Brown fur
on back

Small eyes
(and poor
eyesight)

Strong limbs
for swimming

Pale fur
underneath

Long, coarse
tail with few
hairs – same
length as body

FACT FILE

Size Up to 2 m

Weight 45–175 kg

Habitat Coastal waters of the North Atlantic Ocean

Breeding Adults mate underwater and single pups are born

SUPER FACT

Seals need to breathe in air, but they can hold their breath for up to ten minutes when they dive below water, searching for fish to eat.

PHOTO FILE

Common seals come to land to breed, rest or moult and may form enormous colonies, or groups, of more than 1000 individuals.

MY NOTES & PICTURES

I'VE SEEN A... Juvenile ◯ Adult ◯

COMMON SEAL *Phoca vitulina*

Nearly half of the European population of common seals live around the coast of Britain, usually in sheltered waters. These large mammals often come to land, hauling themselves awkwardly onto rocky shores, mudflats and sand bars. Here, their pups are protected from predators, such as foxes and birds of prey. The common seal is also known as the harbour seal.

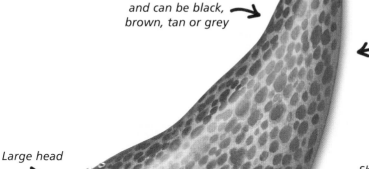

SCALE

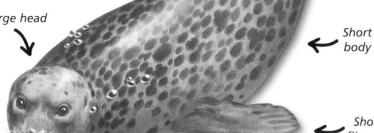

Colour varies and can be black, brown, tan or grey

Every seal has a different pattern on its fur

Large head

Short body

Short flippers

Nostrils form a 'V' shape

MAMMALS

FACT FILE

Size 5–8.2 cm

Weight 5–12 g

Habitat Woodlands, hedgerows, grasslands

Breeding A litter can contain up to ten young and females produce 2–4 litters a year

SUPER FACT

Common shrews don't like company! If they bump into each other they freeze, then squeak and stand up on their hind legs before running away.

PHOTO FILE

This shrew has to eat 80–90 percent of its own body weight in food every 24 hours or it will starve to death.

MY NOTES & PICTURES

I'VE SEEN A... Juvenile Adult

COMMON SHREW   *Sorex araneus*

Common shrews may be one of the **most abundant mammals in Britain.** However, they are so secretive, you may never spot one unless you know where to look. These little furry animals are experts at remaining hidden beneath vegetation, and they have to spend most of their lives looking for food and eating. With a good sense of smell, shrews can detect prey up to 12 cm underground. They are most active at night, and are preyed upon by owls.

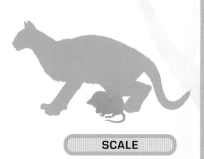

SCALE

Dark brown, soft, silky fur

Pointed snout

Small eyes

Pale fur underneath

FACT FILE

Size 9–12 cm

Weight 20–45 g

Habitat Grasslands

Breeding Females can give birth to their first litter of 3–8 young when only five weeks old

SUPER FACT

Common voles live dangerous lives and few survive more than five months. They are not only hunted by other animals, but males often die after fighting one another.

PHOTO FILE

These glossy-furred voles are huddling together for warmth. The nest is well hidden from predators, inside a burrow.

MY NOTES & PICTURES

I'VE SEEN A... Juvenile Adult ⬭

COMMON VOLE *Microtus arvalis*

At first glance, a vole can easily be mistaken for a rat. However, if they stay still long enough to be identified, their plump bodies and thicker fur are obvious. These animals live in open meadows or fields where they can eat grass or agricultural crops. Common voles dig burrows where they build their nests, sleep and hide stores of food. They are eaten by weasels, stoats, polecats, foxes and birds of prey.

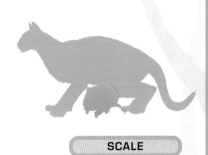

SCALE

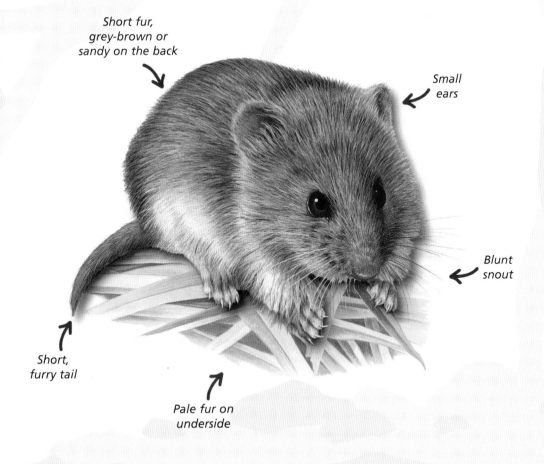

Short fur, grey-brown or sandy on the back

Small ears

Blunt snout

Short, furry tail

Pale fur on underside

IN THE... Garden ○   Park ○   Countryside ○

MAMMALS

FACT FILE

Size Wingspan 24–27 cm

Weight 7–15 g

Habitat Near water

Breeding The bats mate in the autumn and females give birth in summer

SUPER FACT

Like other bats, Daubenton's bat makes sounds that it can use to locate its prey and judge its distance and size. This is called echolocation.

PHOTO FILE

These bats hibernate between September and March or April. The places where animals choose to hibernate are called hibernacula.

MY NOTES & PICTURES

I'VE SEEN A... Juvenile ◯   Adult ◯

DAUBENTON'S BAT *Myotis daubentonii*

These common bats live near sources of water, such as canals, reservoirs and rivers. At twilight they can sometimes be spotted swooping down to the water's surface, chasing insects at speeds of about 25 km/h. Their diet is mostly made up of midges, caddis flies and mayflies. In summer they roost in tree holes, bridges and caves, and up to 200 bats may live in one colony.

SCALE

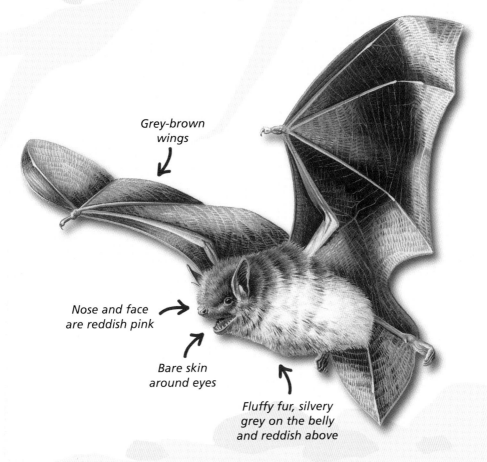

Grey-brown
wings

Nose and face
are reddish pink

Bare skin
around eyes

Fluffy fur, silvery
grey on the belly
and reddish above

MAMMALS

FACT FILE

Size 6–9 cm

Weight 15–30 g

Habitat Woodlands, shrubbery

Breeding Breed from May–October, producing 2–7 young at a time

SUPER FACT

This animal is known for its sleepiness – and that's how it got its name. The 'dor' part comes from the French verb 'dormir', which means 'to sleep'.

PHOTO FILE

Dormice feed on a wide variety of food, including flowers, nuts and insects. Stores of fat in their bodies help them survive the winter.

MY NOTES & PICTURES

I'VE SEEN A... Juvenile Adult ◯

DORMOUSE

Muscardinus avellanarius

Dormice spend up to three-quarters of their lives sleeping, and much of that time is spent in hibernation. A long sleep over winter is a good way to save energy when there is little food around. However, when they are active, dormice are very sprightly and jump, climb and scuttle around. This rodent is also known as the hazel dormouse or common dormouse.

SCALE

Golden fur on back

Large eyes

Paler fur on underside

Long, fluffy tail

FACT FILE

Size 85–100 cm at the shoulder

Weight 30–85 kg

Habitat Woodlands

Breeding Females give birth to a single fawn in June

SUPER FACT

The Normans brought fallow deer to England in the 11th century. Large deer parks were set up in medieval times so members of the royal family could hunt them.

PHOTO FILE

Fallow deer do not grow antlers until they are three years old. Females look like young deer when they lose their antlers in spring.

MY NOTES & PICTURES

I'VE SEEN A... Juvenile ◯ Adult ◯

FALLOW DEER
Dama dama

ost fallow deer live in parks where they are protected, but some live wild. They are particularly active at dawn and dusk, but they spend much of their time grazing. During the mating season, males can become very aggressive and they fight one another to get more does, or females, in their group. Fallow deer are sometimes farmed for their meat, which is called venison.

SCALE

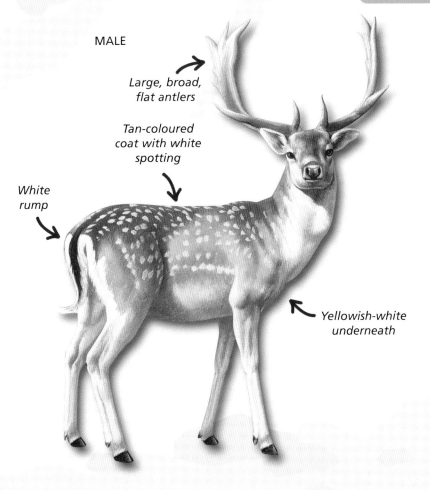

MALE

Large, broad, flat antlers

Tan-coloured coat with white spotting

White rump

Yellowish-white underneath

MAMMALS

FACT FILE

Size 40–60 cm

Weight 2.5–7 kg

Habitat All habitats, especially where people live

Breeding Each year females may have only one or two kittens that survive for 12 months

SUPER FACT

Many small organizations help to care for feral cats by feeding them or providing veterinary care. Few feral cats become pets as they are too scared of people.

PHOTO FILE

Feral cats have to find their own food. When hunting prey, such as birds and mice, they crouch low, waiting for the moment to pounce.

MY NOTES & PICTURES

I'VE SEEN A...　Juvenile ◯　　　Adult ◯

FERAL CAT _Felis catus_

Many feral cats were once unwanted **pets.** They are not a different type of cat to pet cats – they just have a different lifestyle because they live in the wild. They should also not be confused with wildcats, which are a different species. Feral cats mainly have a tabby pattern, rather than the pure colour of pet cats. They live in farms, parks or gardens, often in large groups.

SCALE

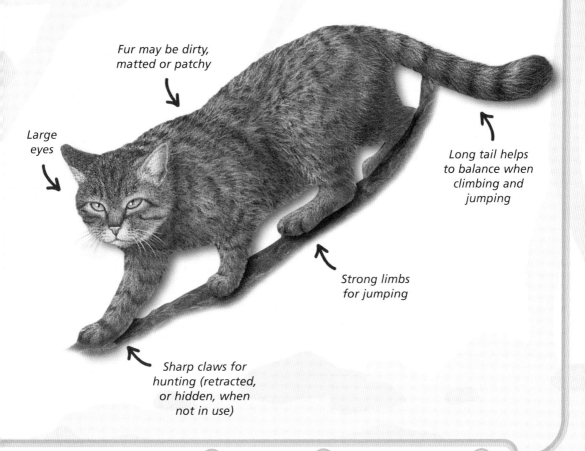

Fur may be dirty, matted or patchy

Large eyes

Long tail helps to balance when climbing and jumping

Strong limbs for jumping

Sharp claws for hunting (retracted, or hidden, when not in use)

FACT FILE

Size 8–13 cm

Weight 15–50 g

Habitat Rough grassland, woodland, fields, hedges

Breeding Breeds from March–October and each litter has 2–7 young

SUPER FACT

One female can have up to five litters a year. If each litter contains five babies, this is a total of 25 babies a year!

PHOTO FILE

Voles are rarely seen as they hide away from predators amongst foliage and leaf litter. They dig burrows to nest in.

MY NOTES & PICTURES

I'VE SEEN A...   Juvenile   ◯   Adult

FIELD VOLE *Microtus agrestis*

Also known as short-tailed voles, field voles are one of Europe's most common mammals, although they are rarely spotted. They mostly live in grassland, scrub, woodland and hedgerows. The diet of field voles is mostly grass, so they live where they can find a plentiful supply. They may come into gardens that border countryside. They have grey-brown fur on their backs and creamy-white fur underneath.

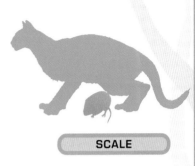

SCALE

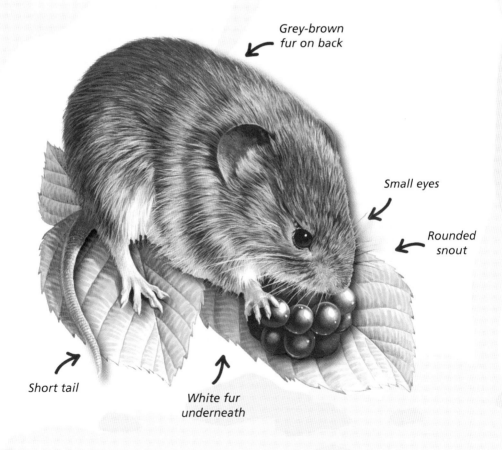

Grey-brown fur on back

Small eyes

Rounded snout

Short tail

White fur underneath

MAMMALS

FACT FILE

Size 5–6 cm

Weight 4–6 g

Habitat Dry grasslands, fields

Breeding 3–7 litters a year, with 1–8 young in each

SUPER FACT

The spherical nests built by pregnant females are very complicated structures. They are woven from grass and can measure 10 cm in diameter.

PHOTO FILE

Tiny harvest mice start breeding when they are just six weeks old, and rarely live to more than six months of age.

MY NOTES & PICTURES

I'VE SEEN A... Juvenile ◯ Adult ◯

HARVEST MOUSE *Micromys minutus*

The European harvest mouse is the **smallest rodent in Britain.** It has an extraordinary tail, which it uses like a fifth limb. A harvest mouse can wrap its tail around grass stems, using it for balance, climbing and grasping. They eat grass, berries, cereals, fruit, insects and seeds. Harvest mice are at risk from pesticides and combine harvesters, but their natural predators include crows, cats and weasels.

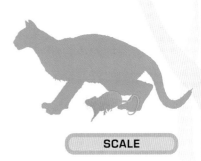

SCALE

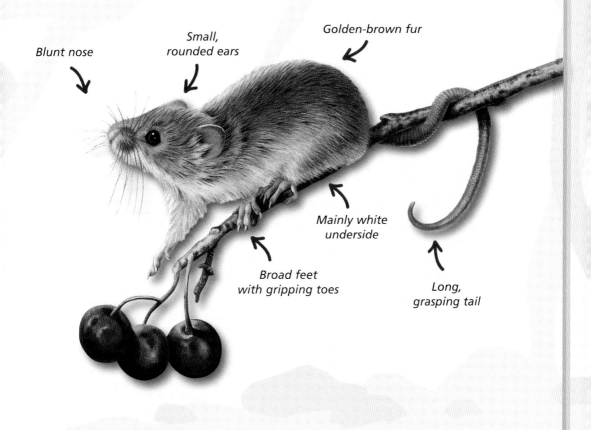

Blunt nose

Small, rounded ears

Golden-brown fur

Mainly white underside

Broad feet with gripping toes

Long, grasping tail

IN THE... Garden ○   Park ○   Countryside ○

MAMMALS

FACT FILE

Size 20–30 cm

Weight 1–2 kg

Habitat Woodlands, farms, parks, gardens, hedges

Breeding Breeds in the spring and 2–7 young are born five weeks later

SUPER FACT

Young hedgehogs are born blind and helpless. Their mother cares for them for four weeks before they can leave the nest.

PHOTO FILE

The average hedgehog is covered in 5000–7000 spines, although there are none on the face, chest or legs. Hedgehogs also have small tails.

MY NOTES & PICTURES

I'VE SEEN A... Juvenile ◯ Adult ◯

HEDGEHOG *Erinaceus europaeus*

These prickly mammals are welcome visitors to gardens, as they eat many pests. Hedgehogs are carnivores and eat slugs, worms, beetles, carrion, eggs and nestlings. They normally live alone and can walk for several kilometres at night as they look for food. These small animals are preyed upon by badgers and foxes. Hedgehogs hibernate from October to April in compost heaps and bonfire piles. They can be injured accidentally by gardeners.

SCALE

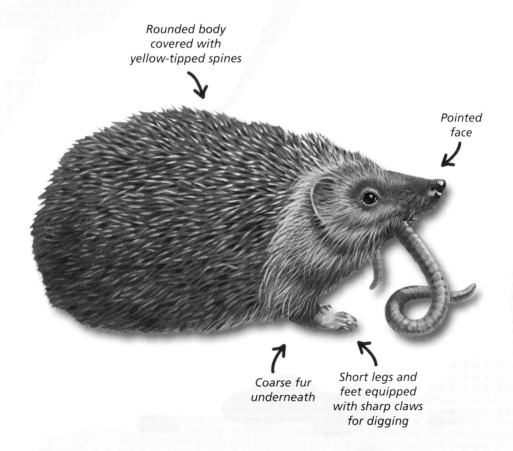

Rounded body covered with yellow-tipped spines

Pointed face

Coarse fur underneath

Short legs and feet equipped with sharp claws for digging

MAMMALS

FACT FILE

Size 11–16 cm

Weight 70–130 g

Habitat Woodlands, fields, parks, gardens

Breeding Breeds from February–June and has litters of 3 or 4 young

SUPER FACT

Moles are well-known for their digging skills. They use their shovel-like forelimbs to scoop earth away to create a tunnel.

PHOTO FILE

Moles live underground. When they dig their way to the surface, they create mounds of earth called molehills.

MY NOTES & PICTURES

I'VE SEEN A... Juvenile Adult ◯

MOLE *Talpa europaea*

It is unusual to see moles as they spend most of their lives underground, digging or sleeping. They have soft, dense, grey-black fur, pink noses, whiskers, and very small eyes. They eat earthworms and insect grubs, which they find using their excellent senses of smell and hearing. They store hundreds of worms in underground larders so they have a ready supply of food.

SCALE

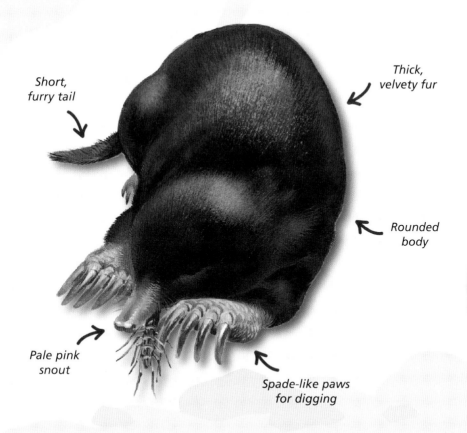

Short, furry tail

Thick, velvety fur

Rounded body

Pale pink snout

Spade-like paws for digging

FACT FILE

Size 45–66 cm

Weight 2–6 kg

Habitat Forests, moorlands

Breeding Between 1–4 litters are produced a year, with 1–5 young in each

SUPER FACT

A female mountain hare can produce up to 25 youngsters, or leverets, in a breeding season. If she lives for nine years, she could have several hundred offspring!

PHOTO FILE

Hares keep their fur clean with regular washing and preening. This helps to keep them free of parasites.

MY NOTES & PICTURES

I'VE SEEN A... Juvenile ◯ Adult ◯

MOUNTAIN HARE *Lepus timidus*

Unlike its cousins, the brown hare and the rabbit, the mountain hare is native to Britain but is found only in Scotland and northern regions of England. These hares are most likely to be spotted alone, in the early morning or at dusk. Occasionally a group may feed together. They eat grasses, heather, rushes and herbs, and are preyed upon by foxes, stoats, cats and birds of prey. The mountain hare is also known as the blue hare or white hare.

SCALE

Ears tipped with black

Coat is brown in summer, white in winter

Slender, agile body

Tail stays white throughout the year

Long legs and large feet

MAMMALS

FACT FILE

Size Wingspan 32–45 cm

Weight 20–40 g

Habitat Woodlands, parks, gardens

Breeding A single young bat is born in June or early July

SUPER FACT

Noctules huddle together during their winter hibernations to keep warm. However, in very cold weather, half of all the bats in a colony may freeze to death.

PHOTO FILE

Despite what many people believe, bats are not blind and many of them, like this noctule bat, have very good eyesight.

MY NOTES & PICTURES

I'VE SEEN A... Juvenile ◯ Adult ◯

NOCTULE BAT

Nyctalus noctula

Noctule bats emerge from their resting places in the early evening, before the sun has completely set. They hunt for insects, such as moths and beetles. They are fast fliers and can dart around, diving or changing direction swiftly. It is harder to find noctules in the winter, as they either migrate south to warmer places or hibernate. They can live to 12 years of age and are found in England and Wales only.

SCALE

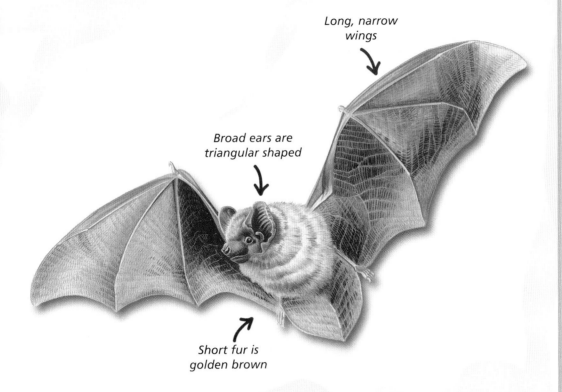

Long, narrow wings

Broad ears are triangular shaped

Short fur is golden brown

FACT FILE

Size 55–80 cm

Weight 7–10 kg

Habitat Unpolluted rivers, lakes and coasts

Breeding Throughout the year, 2–3 cubs are born at a time

SUPER FACT

Otter cubs need a helping hand to learn how to fish. Their mother catches a fish and then releases it in front of the cubs, so they can practise capturing it for themselves.

PHOTO FILE

An otter's thick fur traps a layer of air next to the skin, keeping the animal warm and dry when it swims.

MY NOTES & PICTURES

I'VE SEEN A... Juvenile Adult ◯

OTTER *Lutra lutra*

Sighting an otter by a riverbank is a rare treat. These animals are very shy and likely to disappear beneath the water's surface when they are disturbed. They mostly feed on fish, but they will also eat water birds or frogs. Otters find it hard to survive in polluted water and this has affected their numbers in recent years. They have also been hunted for their fur and to stop them eating fish.

SCALE

Smooth, brown fur

Long, slender body

Pale on underside

Short legs

Webbed feet

Thick tail

MAMMALS

FACT FILE

Size 45–55 cm
Weight 1–2.2 kg
Habitat Woodlands, cliffs
Breeding 1–5 cubs born in spring

SUPER FACT

Pine martens were brought close to extinction during the 18th and 19th centuries. They were killed for their fur and to stop them preying upon chickens and game birds.

PHOTO FILE

Young pine martens spend six weeks in their den before they venture out. They stay with their mothers until they are six months old.

MY NOTES & PICTURES

I'VE SEEN A... Juvenile Adult

PINE MARTEN *Martes martes*

Pine martens are nocturnal mammals, which means they are most active at night and usually sleep during the day. They make their dens in tree holes, old squirrel nests and rocky crevices. They eat a wide range of food, depending on what is available – from rodents and birds to eggs, beetles and berries. They are excellent climbers but hunt on the ground. Pine martens live in very few areas of Britain outside of Scotland.

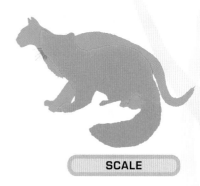

SCALE

Big ears

Large eyes

Pointed muzzle

Creamy yellow patch of fur on chest

Dark–light-brown fur

Long, fluffy tail

IN THE... Garden ◯   Park ◯   Countryside ◯

MAMMALS

FACT FILE

Size Wingspan 19–25 cm

Weight 3–10 g

Habitat Almost all habitats, except very open places

Breeding Males mate with 8–10 females in autumn and each female has 1–2 young

SUPER FACT

In Britain, female pipistrelles usually give birth to just one young, but in central Europe, twins are much more common.

PHOTO FILE

Bats are the only mammals that can fly. In the evening, pipistrelles are the first bats to appear as they hunt for insects.

MY NOTES & PICTURES

I'VE SEEN A... Juvenile Adult ○

PIPISTRELLE BAT

Pipistrellus pipistrellus

Pipistrelles are the smallest and most **common bats in the UK.** They are unlikely to be spotted in winter, but during summer they swoop and dive, with a characteristic jerky flight, over gardens. They roost in buildings, and can squeeze through tiny gaps to find somewhere sheltered and dry to rest. They feed on flying insects, and one bat can eat more than 3000 insects in one night.

SCALE

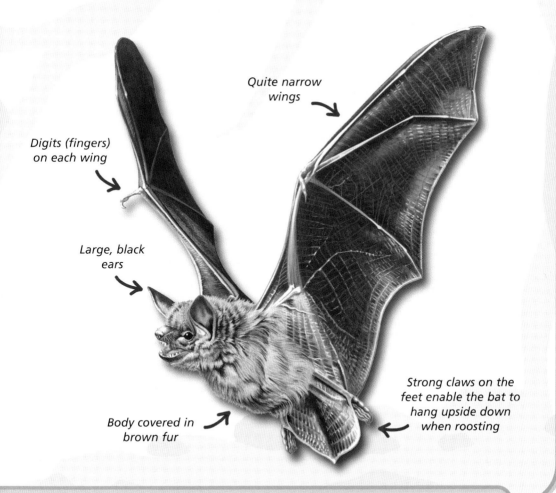

Quite narrow wings

Digits (fingers) on each wing

Large, black ears

Strong claws on the feet enable the bat to hang upside down when roosting

Body covered in brown fur

IN THE... Garden ◯ Park ◯ Countryside ◯

MAMMALS

FACT FILE

Size 35–51 cm

Weight 0.7–1.5 kg

Habitat Marshes, woods, riverbanks

Breeding A single litter of 3–7 young born in May or June

SUPER FACT

In the times of Queen Elizabeth I, about 450 years ago, polecats were regarded as bloodthirsty vermin, or pests. They were hunted mercilessly and nearly became extinct.

PHOTO FILE

Polecats are territorial. They defend an area of land for themselves and leave scent markings to keep other animals away.

MY NOTES & PICTURES

I'VE SEEN A...   Juvenile   Adult ◯

POLECAT *Mustela putorius*

Polecats are easy to identify because they have characteristic markings on their faces. However, they are hard to spot because they only come out during the day when they are struggling to find food, and are normally active at dusk or night. Polecats are carnivores, which means they eat meat. They hunt rabbits, rodents, frogs, toads and birds, but will eat insects too. These mammals are found in England and Wales.

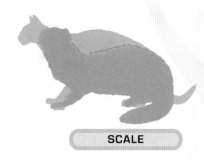

SCALE

Broad head

Black, mask-like markings

Slender body

Dark coat

Short legs

MAMMALS

FACT FILE

Size 4–6 cm

Weight 4–6 g

Habitat Grassland, fields, hedges, farms, gardens, parks

Breeding Breeds from April–October and 4–7 young are born 23 days later

SUPER FACT

Pygmy shrews rarely live for more than one year. They may not survive harsh winters and they are preyed upon by large mammals, such as cats, foxes and stoats.

PHOTO FILE

Pygmy shrews have to eat every few hours or they starve to death. They feed on insects, worms and carrion (dead animals).

MY NOTES & PICTURES

I'VE SEEN A... Juvenile ◯ Adult ◯

PYGMY SHREW *Sorex minutus*

These small, rodent-like mammals are often found near compost heaps in gardens. Pygmy shrews run away quickly when disturbed, making it difficult to identify them for sure – at first glance, they look like young mice or rats. Pygmy shrews are common visitors to gardens and they are the UK's smallest mammal.

SCALE

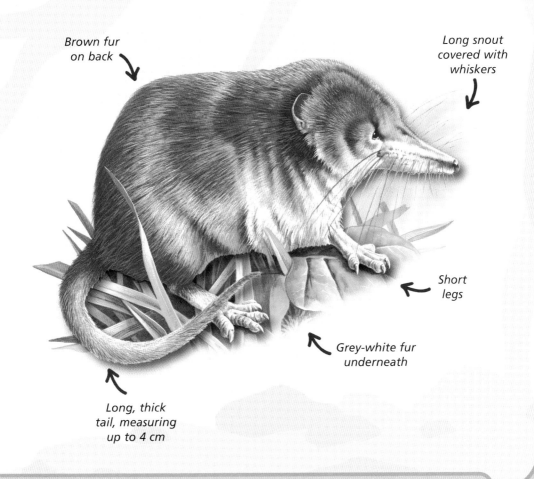

Brown fur on back

Long snout covered with whiskers

Short legs

Grey-white fur underneath

Long, thick tail, measuring up to 4 cm

MAMMALS

FACT FILE

Size 34–50 cm

Weight 1.3–2.6 kg

Habitat Scrubland, rocky areas, hedgerows, fields

Breeding Up to ten young are born in a litter each month from February–August

SUPER FACT

Myxomatosis is a rabbit disease that reached Britain in the 1950s. It killed nearly all the wild British rabbits. The disease still exists, but not to such a deadly degree.

PHOTO FILE

Rabbits are preyed upon by other animals, so they must remain alert and on the lookout at all times, looking, listening and sniffing.

MY NOTES & PICTURES

I'VE SEEN A... Juvenile ◯　　　Adult ◯

RABBIT   *Oryctolagus cuniculus*

The European rabbit was brought to Britain by the Normans in the 11th century to provide fur and meat. Since then, they have settled so well that many people regard them as pests. Rabbits eat plant matter, such as grass, crops, cereals and young trees. They live in burrows that connect together to make a warren. Young rabbits are called kittens.

SCALE

Long ears with black tips (but shorter than hares' ears)

Eyes on either side of head

Coat can be grey, brown, sandy yellow or black

White underneath

MAMMALS

FACT FILE

Size Up to 1.2 m at the shoulder

Weight Up to 225 kg

Habitat Grassland, woodland, moors

Breeding Single fawns are born in May or June

SUPER FACT

In autumn, stags fight to mate with the most females. During this time, which is called 'the rut', they roar, lock antlers, push and twist. Fights can cause injury or death.

PHOTO FILE

The new antlers of a deer are covered in a soft, sensitive coating called velvet. This is rubbed off when the antlers are fully grown.

MY NOTES & PICTURES

I'VE SEEN A... Juvenile ◯ Adult ◯

RED DEER *Cervus elaphus*

Red deer are the largest land-living mammals that are native to Britain, but they are mostly restricted to parts of Scotland. The females are called hinds, the males are called stags and the young are called fawns. Red deer stags have the largest antlers of any British deer, and they can reach an impressive one metre in width. Stags and hinds often spend their time in separate groups, coming together only at breeding time.

SCALE

MALE

Multi-branched antlers

Rump has a patch of cream-coloured fur

Reddish-brown coat in summer, dull brown in winter

FACT FILE

Size 50–80 cm

Weight 2–7 kg

Habitat Fields, scrubland, gardens, parks, along railways

Breeding Mate mid-winter and 4–5 cubs are born 52 days later

SUPER FACT

Foxes are secretive animals, except during breeding season in winter, when they become very noisy.

PHOTO FILE

Cubs are born completely blind in early spring. When they are a few months old, they can often be seen playing in gardens.

MY NOTES & PICTURES

I'VE SEEN A... Juvenile ◯ Adult ◯

RED FOX *Vulpes vulpes*

Once mainly found in the countryside, red foxes are now widespread in towns and cities – where they have discovered a new source of food. They often scavenge from rubbish bins and will eat almost any food they find lying around. Females are called vixens and are smaller than males, which are called dogs. Foxes are most active at night, especially at dawn and dusk.

SCALE

Reddish-brown fur (may be mangy, dirty or patchy)

Black fur on ears

Long, thick tail, known as a 'brush'

White chest and throat

Black fur on legs

MAMMALS

FACT FILE

Size 20–24 cm

Weight 280–350 g

Habitat Conifer woodlands

Breeding Mating occurs January–March and a litter of young (normally three) is born around 40 days later

SUPER FACT

The number of red squirrels in Britain has dropped dramatically. This is largely because they have to compete with grey squirrels for food.

PHOTO FILE

Like their grey cousins, red squirrels usually eat in trees, where they are safer from predators. They store food in crevices and cracks in bark.

MY NOTES & PICTURES

I'VE SEEN A... Juvenile Adult ◯

RED SQUIRREL *Sciurus vulgaris*

These squirrels are smaller than their grey cousins. They are much harder to spot nowadays because there are only a few places in Britain where they have been able to survive. They usually live in woodlands with conifer trees, where they can chew on pine cones and nibble pine seeds. They also eat leaves, fruit, buds and insects. Red squirrels build nests, called dreys, which are made from a frame of twigs, lined with soft plants.

SCALE

Bushy tail

Tufted ears in winter

Buff or cream-coloured underneath

Colour varies from russet brown to dark brown, or grey in winter

FACT FILE

Size Up to 75 cm at the shoulder

Weight Up to 25 kg

Habitat Grassland, woodland, moors

Breeding 1–3 fawns (called kids) are born in May or June

SUPER FACT

Young fawns are left alone all day while their parents feed. Their spotted coats help them hide from predators. At six weeks, they follow their mothers everywhere.

PHOTO FILE

Young roe deer are called kids. They have fluffy coats with white spots for the first six weeks of life, eventually turning reddish grey.

MY NOTES & PICTURES

I'VE SEEN A... Juvenile Adult ○

ROE DEER *Capreolus capreolus*

This is an elegant, small deer that **originally comes from Scotland, but has been introduced to other parts of Britain.** It is easiest to see roe deer at dawn and dusk when they are less likely to be resting or hiding. They lose their antlers between October and January. When the new antlers grow, they are covered in soft 'velvet', which provides blood to help them develop.

SCALE

MALE

Male's antlers usually have three points

Black muzzle band

White chin and throat patches

Large, white rump

Reddish fur in summer, grey-brown-black in winter

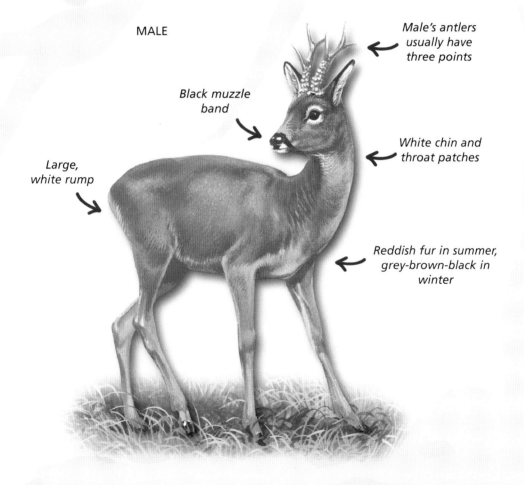

IN THE... Garden ◯ Park ◯ Countryside ◯

FACT FILE

Size 23–30 cm

Weight 1–4 kg

Habitat Farms, woodland, parks, grasslands, scrubland

Breeding Mates in the summer and a litter of 6–12 is born in the spring

SUPER FACT

In winter, stoats were once hunted for their ermine pelts (fur), which were used for stoles and robes worn by royalty and judges. Nowadays, artificial fur is used.

PHOTO FILE

Stoats are carnivores. They hunt both day and night and their prey includes voles, mice, birds, rabbits and hares.

MY NOTES & PICTURES

I'VE SEEN A...   Juvenile ◯   Adult ◯

STOAT

Mustela erminea

These mammals are closely related to weasels, pine martens, otters, minks and badgers. However, stoats are larger than weasels and have reddish-brown fur. In northern parts of the UK, their fur turns white in winter. They can climb trees, swim and jump. Stoats use their excellent sense of smell to find their prey, which they kill with a single bite to the back of the neck. Thanks to their long and slender bodies, stoats can chase their prey into burrows.

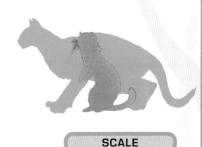

SCALE

Small eyes and ears

Reddish-brown fur on back

White fur underneath

Black-tipped tail

Long, slender body

IN THE... Garden ◯ Park ◯ Countryside ◯

MAMMALS

FACT FILE

Size 6.5–9.5 cm

Weight 12–19 g

Habitat Damp woodlands, ponds, rivers

Breeding Up to three litters of 3–14 young are born in summer

SUPER FACT

Water shrews' teeth contain iron. This hard metal makes the teeth tough and less likely to wear down, despite chewing and gnawing. It gives them a red tinge at the tips.

PHOTO FILE

Mammals that swim underwater, such as this shrew, have thick fur that keeps them dry and warm, but they cannot breathe underwater.

MY NOTES & PICTURES

I'VE SEEN A...   Juvenile ◯   Adult ◯

WATER SHREW *Neomys fodiens*

This is the largest of the three British shrews and it lives near streams, rivers and ponds. It particularly likes watercress beds. Water shrews do not hibernate and are most active at night, when they dive underwater in search of small creatures to eat. Their fur is waterproof and holds bubbles of air, giving this small mammal a silvery appearance when it dives underwater.

SCALE

Black fur on back

White tufts of fur near eyes and ears

Long, sensitive snout

Long tail

Whitish fur underneath

MAMMALS

FACT FILE

Size 14–22.5 cm

Weight 150–300 g

Habitat Waterside vegetation, near ponds or streams

Breeding Up to five litters are born in summer, each with 3–7 young, which are called pups

SUPER FACT

Young female water voles can force their mothers to leave the burrows by hitting them with their tails or even boxing them with their forefeet!

PHOTO FILE

Water voles can stop water from getting into their ears by closing them with special flaps of skin. They spend most of the day eating.

MY NOTES & PICTURES

I'VE SEEN A...   Juvenile ◯   Adult

WATER VOLE *Arvicola terrestris*

These voles were once commonplace in Britain, but their numbers have dropped dramatically in recent years. It is thought that this is because their riverside habitats have been destroyed or polluted, and because American minks hunt them – causing their extinction in some areas. These mammals eat plants growing by the water's edge and are excellent swimmers. Water voles are also known as water rats.

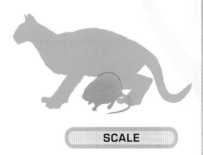

SCALE

Thick fur can be black, brown or reddish-brown in colour

Small ears

Short tail, covered in hair

Rounded face with blunt snout

MAMMALS

FACT FILE

Size 15–25 cm

Weight 50–100 g

Habitat Woodland, farms, gardens

Breeding Mates from spring to autumn and 3–8 young are born after seven weeks

SUPER FACT

Weasels sometimes leap around strangely. It was thought they did this to confuse their prey, but it actually may be due to a worm that lives in weasels' noses.

PHOTO FILE

In northern Europe, the weasel's fur turns white to provide camouflage in the snow. It is then known as the weasel form of ermine.

MY NOTES & PICTURES

I'VE SEEN A...   Juvenile   Adult ◯

WEASEL *Mustela nivalis*

Found in woods, farms and large gardens, weasels are active both at night and during the day. They sleep in burrows that have been abandoned by badgers or rabbits. Weasels live alone and mark their territory with strong scent. They are busy mammals and need to eat regularly to maintain their energy levels – they cannot survive more than 24 hours without food.

SCALE

Small, flattened head

Long, slender body

Brown fur on back

White fur underneath

Short legs

IN THE... Garden ◯ Park ◯ Countryside ◯

MAMMALS

FACT FILE

Size 8–10 cm

Weight 13–27 g

Habitat Widespread in most habitats

Breeding Up to seven litters are born every year, each with 2–9 young

SUPER FACT

If wood mice are caught by other mammals or birds of prey, they can lose the skin of their tails – allowing them to escape. The rest of the tail soon dies and falls off.

PHOTO FILE

Wood mice build their nests in underground tunnels or hollow logs. They huddle together for warmth, but do not hibernate.

MY NOTES & PICTURES

I'VE SEEN A... Juvenile ◯ Adult ◯

WOOD MOUSE
Apodemus sylvaticus

Although wood mice are normally **nocturnal, they may be spotted during daylight hours at breeding times.** They eat a wide range of food, including moss, seeds, small insects and nuts. Males are very aggressive and often fight one another to protect their territories. They have even been known to kill young mice. The wood mouse is also known as the long-tailed field mouse.

SCALE

Brown or chestnut fur

Large ears and eyes

White or grey belly

Tail as long as the body

FACT FILE

Size 9–12.5 cm

Weight 15–45 g

Habitat Woodlands, gardens, orchards

Breeding About three litters are born every summer, of 2–11 young each time

SUPER FACT

When the young are born they are blind and helpless. They open their eyes when they are about 16 days old, and just five days later they are completely independent.

PHOTO FILE

Rodents, like this yellow-necked mouse, have strong front teeth that grow throughout their lives. They can tackle tough food like nuts.

MY NOTES & PICTURES

I'VE SEEN A... Juvenile ◯ Adult ◯

YELLOW-NECKED MOUSE _Apodemus flavicollis_

It is easy to confuse wood mice and yellow-necked mice as they are very similar in size and appearance. The only distinguishing mark is the patch of yellow fur on a yellow-necked mouse's neck, but this is often difficult to spot – especially as mice are fast-movers! Yellow-necked mice are mostly nocturnal and are excellent climbers. They eat seeds, fruit, buds and seedlings. These mice live in some regions of England and Wales.

SCALE

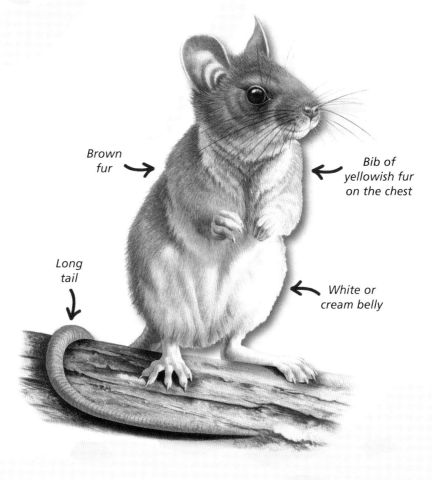

Brown fur →

← Bib of yellowish fur on the chest

Long tail ↓

← White or cream belly

IN THE... Garden ◯ Park ◯ Countryside ◯

FACT FILE

Size 40–43 cm
Wingspan 67–77 cm
Call Loud 'kloot' call
Habitat Estuaries, coasts, shores
Breeding 3–4 pale buff eggs
laid April–June, hatching
around 24 days later

SUPER FACT

Chicks face a difficult few months
after hatching and if the weather
is bad many of them may die. Few
avocets live beyond seven years of
age, but one has lived to 24 years.

PHOTO FILE

An avocet uses its long and slender bill to
root around in thick, sludgy mud, searching
for small animals to catch and eat.

MY NOTES & PICTURES

I'VE SEEN IT... Eating ○   Flying ○   Nesting ○

AVOCET *Recurvirostra avosetta*

Beautiful, elegant wading birds, avocets **are found in coastal habitats, especially in eastern England.** They have distinctive black-and-white plumage, long legs and unusually long beaks. They use these to sweep through mud, searching for insects, shelled animals and worms to eat. Avocets became extinct in Britain in the 19th century, but they were successfully reintroduced to England in the 1940s. Now they are the symbol for the RSPB (Royal Society for the Protection of Birds).

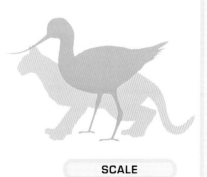

SCALE

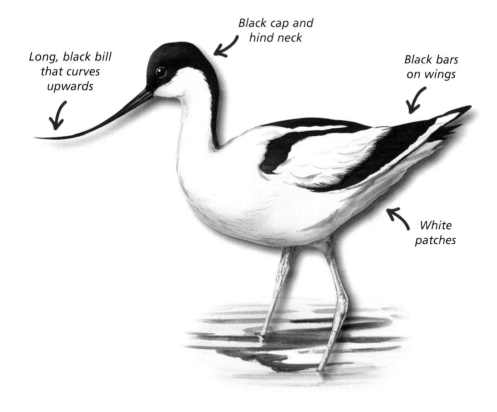

Black cap and
hind neck

Long, black bill
that curves
upwards

Black bars
on wings

White
patches

FACT FILE

Size 90–110 cm
Wingspan 1.3–1.8 m
Call Deep loud 'ah-ronk'
Habitat Coasts, marshes, lakes
Breeding 5–6 eggs are laid in the spring, hatching around 25 days later

SUPER FACT

The edges of a Canada goose's bill are lined with special 'teeth' called lamellae. These are used to cut grass or other vegetation.

PHOTO FILE

When Canada geese fly in groups their flocks often form a V-shape in the sky. They start to fly when they are 6–9 weeks old.

MY NOTES & PICTURES

I'VE SEEN IT... Eating ◯ Flying ◯ Nesting ◯

CANADA GOOSE
Branta canadensis

These geese originally came to Britain
from North America. They quickly settled
in and are now established all over the
country, except in the most northern areas.
They are often considered a nuisance because
they gather together in large, noisy groups.
Males and females form lifelong pairs – this
behaviour is described as monogamy, which
means having just one mating partner. A pair
stays together to look after the eggs and the
young, which are called goslings.

SCALE

Black bill

Body is
swan-shaped

White
chinstrap

White patch
under tail

Pale
breast

Black
legs

AT THE...   Coast ◯   Lake ◯   Marsh ◯

FACT FILE

Size 10–11 cm
Wingspan 15–21 cm
Habitat Woodlands, parks
Call 'Hweet' or 'chip-chap'
Breeding 5–6 eggs laid from April–July, hatching about 14 days later

SUPER FACT

Young chiffchaffs stay in the nest for about two weeks before they are ready to fly. If any animal approaches them in the meantime, they will try to attack it.

PHOTO FILE

Young chiffchaffs have brighter, longer stripes of yellow on their eyes. These birds bob their tails downwards when they are perching.

MY NOTES & PICTURES

I'VE SEEN IT... Eating ◯   Flying ◯   Nesting ◯

CHIFFCHAFF *Phylloscopus collybita*

Chiffchaffs visit Britain in the summer.
However, in southern England and
Ireland, some of them have given up
migrating in the winter and manage to
survive our coldest months. These little birds
are hard to spot because their olive-brown
plumage hides them well in the vegetation.
They are likely to be found close to water.
Chiffchaffs eat insects and spiders that they
find amongst leaves and flowers, and they
are sometimes known as leaf warblers.

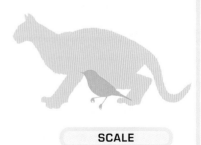

SCALE

*Pale stripe
over eye*

*Olive-brown
plumage on
back and head*

*Short
wingtips*

*Thin,
dark legs*

IN THE... Garden ◯ Park ◯ Countryside ◯

97

BIRDS

FACT FILE

Size 32–33 cm
Wingspan 82–95 cm
Call 'kreee-yar' or 'kik kik keer'
Habitat Coasts, rivers, reservoirs
Breeding Up to four eggs are
laid around May, hatching
about three weeks later

SUPER FACT

These birds have long bodies and
are elegant in flight. On land,
however, they move awkwardly,
because of their short legs.

PHOTO FILE

These water-loving birds build their nests
in sand or dry earth near coasts. They breed
in large groups, or colonies.

MY NOTES & PICTURES

I'VE SEEN IT... Eating ◯ Flying ◯ Nesting ◯

COMMON TERN   *Sterna hirundo*

The common tern is often seen over rivers, hovering and swooping as it feeds. Elegant, but aggressive, this bird is seen across Britain in the summer. During the autumn it migrates to warmer climates, returning in spring. It nests in noisy colonies and flies, often to sea, in search of food. Common terns are light and graceful in flight and can travel for many kilometres before tiring and returning to land. When they spot fish below them, terns plunge-dive into the water in pursuit of their prey.

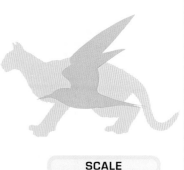

SCALE

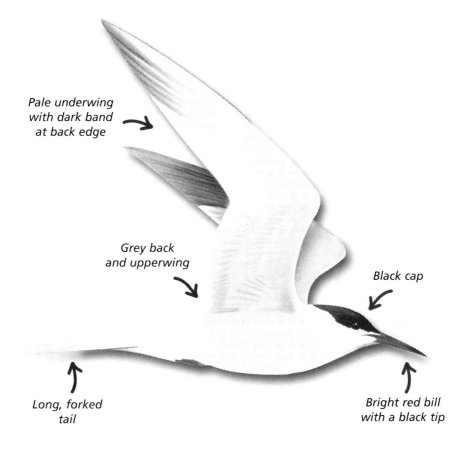

Pale underwing with dark band at back edge

Grey back and upperwing

Black cap

Long, forked tail

Bright red bill with a black tip

AT THE...   Coast ○   River ○   Reservoir ○

BIRDS

FACT FILE

Size 90 cm
Wingspan 1.3–1.6 m
Call Growling and cackling
Habitat Coastal areas,
estuaries, reservoirs
Breeding 3–4 eggs
are laid in April

SUPER FACT

When cormorants perch to dry
themselves they have an unusual
body position, or stance. They
stand up straight with their wings
half open and their neck upright.

PHOTO FILE

Cormorants use sticks or seaweed to build
their bulky, messy nests. The nests are
usually built in trees or on cliff edges.

MY NOTES & PICTURES

I'VE SEEN IT... Eating ◯ Flying ◯ Nesting ◯

CORMORANT *Phalacrocorax carbo*

Cormorants are unusual looking water birds, with angular bodies and dark feathers. They are superb swimmers and live all over Britain in watery habitats, especially by the coast. When a cormorant catches a fish it brings it to the water's surface and shakes it vigorously, before swallowing it. Cormorants have large webbed feet that they use for swimming and for hatching their eggs, which they hold between the top of their feet and their warm bodies.

SCALE

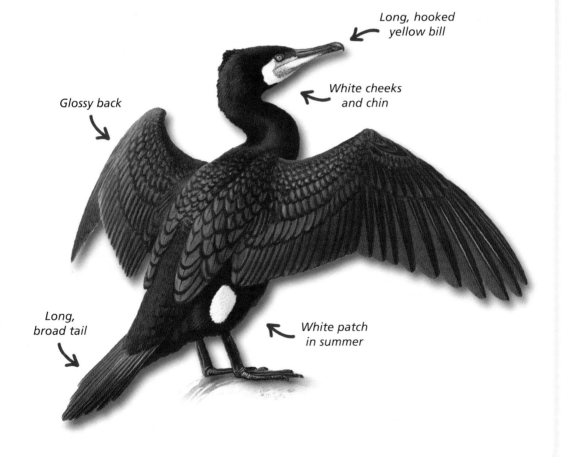

Long, hooked
yellow bill

White cheeks
and chin

Glossy back

Long,
broad tail

White patch
in summer

BIRDS

FACT FILE

Size 32–34 cm
Wingspan 55–65 cm
Call 'Cuc-oo'
Habitat Woods, farmland, heaths, moors
Breeding 1–25 eggs are laid every spring

SUPER FACT

When a cuckoo egg hatches, the young calls loudly. The owners of the nest take on the difficult task of feeding and caring for the large and demanding chick.

PHOTO FILE

Young cuckoos can be identified by the white and black bars on their brown backs. They also have wide tails with black bars.

MY NOTES & PICTURES

I'VE SEEN IT... Eating ◯   Flying ◯   Nesting ◯

CUCKOO *Cuculus canorus*

The cuckoo is best known for its distinctive call, which says its name. When the cuckoo is heard singing, it is a sign that spring is on its way. These medium sized birds spend the winters in warmer places, but visit Britain for the summer months and are found all over the country. When the female is ready to breed, she lays her eggs in other birds' nests (especially those of dunnocks, meadow pipits and reed warblers), and throws the other birds' eggs out of the nest.

SCALE

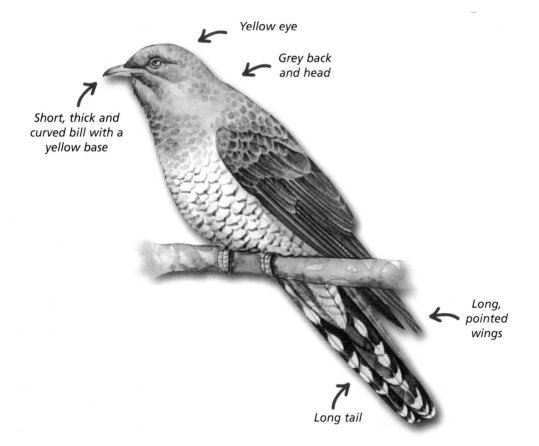

Yellow eye

Grey back and head

Short, thick and curved bill with a yellow base

Long, pointed wings

Long tail

BIRDS

FACT FILE

Size 50–60 cm
Wingspan 80–100 cm
Call Long slow 'cur-loo'
or louder 'whoy'
Habitat Coastal areas, estuaries
Breeding Four eggs are laid
in spring, then incubated for
one month before hatching

SUPER FACT

Curlews use their unusually long,
slender bills to probe the soft
mud in search of small animals,
such as worms, starfish, crabs
and other shelled animals to eat.

PHOTO FILE

Curlews are the largest of all wading birds
in Europe. They are most common around
estuaries and coasts in January and February.

MY NOTES & PICTURES

I'VE SEEN IT... Eating   ◯   Flying   ◯   Nesting   ◯

CURLEW *Numenius arquata*

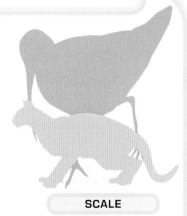

SCALE

Some curlews live permanently in Britain, and can be spotted in coastal areas and other watery habitats throughout the year. Others spend the winter here, and return to Scandinavia when spring arrives. These waders are famous for their beautiful spring song, which has been described as eerie and can be heard at night as well as in the day. Curlews often gather together in large numbers to feed, particularly at the mud flats on estuaries.

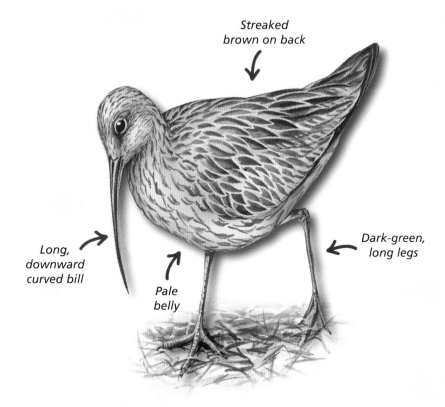

Streaked brown on back

Long, downward curved bill

Pale belly

Dark-green, long legs

AT THE...   **Coast**   **Estuary**

FACT FILE

Size 22–27 cm
Wingspan 39–42 cm
Call Loud 'chack-chack'
Habitat Woodland, heaths, farms, hedges, gardens
Breeding 5–6 eggs from April–July

SUPER FACT

Fieldfares migrate to the UK in winter, but they spend the rest of the year in Scandinavia where they breed. Nowadays, fewer fieldfares are seen in the UK.

PHOTO FILE

Fieldfares feed on seeds, berries and insects, including snails and worms. Hawthorn hedges laden with berries are favourite feeding areas.

MY NOTES & PICTURES

I'VE SEEN IT... Eating ○ Flying ○ Nesting ○

FIELDFARE *Turdus pilaris*

One of the largest types of thrush, fieldfares are social birds. They are often seen hopping along the ground. They visit gardens when they cannot find food in open fields and hedgerows. During autumn and winter, they can occasionally be seen eating ripe fruit that has fallen from trees. Fieldfares usually feed, fly and roost together in flocks.

SCALE

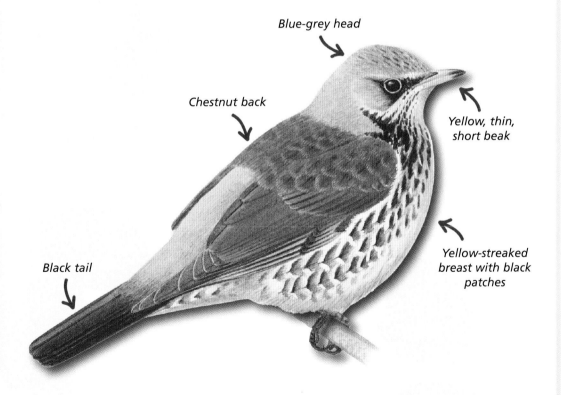

Blue-grey head

Chestnut back

Yellow, thin, short beak

Black tail

Yellow-streaked breast with black patches

FACT FILE

Size 22–33 cm
Wingspan 34–42 cm
Call Sharp, short 'tchak'
Habitat Woodlands,
scrub, gardens
Breeding 4–7 white eggs,
from April–June

SUPER FACT

Woodpeckers make a characteristic drumming noise with their beaks on trees. They look for bugs in the cracks in bark. They have very long tongues for picking up food.

PHOTO FILE

These distinctive birds can perch upright on tree trunks, using their strong claws to keep a grip while they look for food.

MY NOTES & PICTURES

I'VE SEEN IT... Eating ◯ Flying ◯ Nesting ◯

GREAT SPOTTED WOODPECKER *Dendrocopos major*

Boldly coloured, great spotted woodpeckers are black and white, with red rumps. Males also have a red splash on the nape of the neck. Youngsters look similar, but the colours are less bold. They are the size of a blackbird, and the largest of the woodpeckers found in the UK. They live in woodlands, parks and gardens with large trees, and scurry across tree trunks looking for insects to eat.

SCALE

MALE

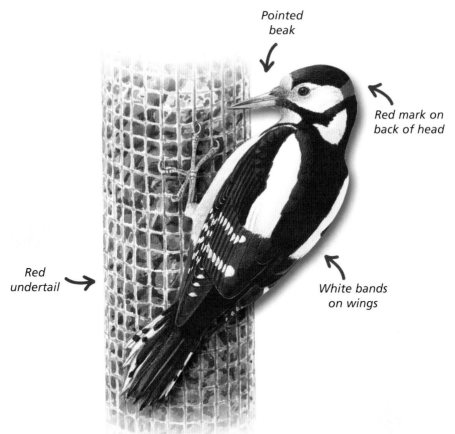

Pointed beak

Red mark on back of head

Red undertail

White bands on wings

BIRDS

FACT FILE

Size 14 cm
Wingspan 22–25 cm
Call Very varied, e.g. 'chink', 'seetoo', 'tui-tui'
Habitat Parks, gardens
Breeding Five or more eggs are laid from April

SUPER FACT

Great tits originally lived in woodlands but they have been drawn to gardens and parks by the food available in these new habitats.

PHOTO FILE

Feeding a brood of youngsters is a hard task for any parent bird. The young are given food that the parent has stored in its stomach.

MY NOTES & PICTURES

I'VE SEEN IT... Eating ◯   Flying ◯   Nesting ◯

GREAT TIT *Parus major*

The energetic and sprightly great tit is a common sight on a bird table, where it fights off other birds to get a bigger portion of food. It is the largest of all British tits, but is still very agile and acrobatic in its flying and perching skills, and can even swing upside down. Great tits have powerful bills that can be used to break tough nuts, but they can eat a wide variety of food, including insects, berries, nuts and seeds.

SCALE

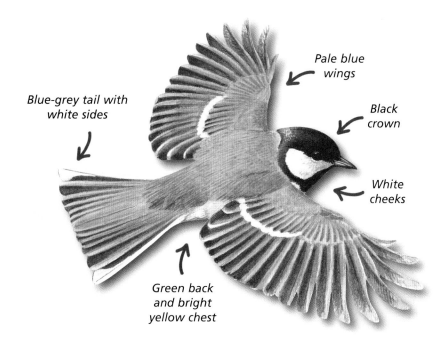

Pale blue wings

Black crown

Blue-grey tail with white sides

White cheeks

Green back and bright yellow chest

BIRDS

FACT FILE

Size 90–100 cm
Wingspan 1.75–1.95 m
Call Rattling and croaking
Habitat Coasts, rivers,
ponds, lakes, marshes
Breeding 4–5 eggs laid
in spring

SUPER FACT

Herons often struggle to survive
long, cold winters. Some British
birds have been found to have
'holidayed' in warmer places
for the winter.

PHOTO FILE

This grey heron has caught a fish, which it
will swallow whole, after flipping it round so
it slides head-first down the bird's throat.

MY NOTES & PICTURES

I'VE SEEN IT... Eating ◯   Flying ◯   Nesting ◯

GREY HERON *Ardea cinerea*

Grey herons are common British water
birds. They make a familiar sight when
they stand patiently waiting on the edge of
a shallow lake or river. These birds either stalk
their prey with very slow movements, or they
wait – motionless – before striking with speed.
They normally eat fish, frogs, worms, insects
and small mammals. Grey herons have been
known to visit garden ponds and hungrily
devour all the fish within.

SCALE

*Black crest
feathers
on head*

*Yellow,
dagger-like
bill*

*Large,
rounded wings*

*White, S-shaped
neck with black
stripe*

*Long, orange-
yellow legs*

AT THE...   River ◯   Lake ◯   Estuary ◯

BIRDS

FACT FILE

Size 55–67 cm
Wingspan 1.3–1.6 m
Call Loud 'kyow', 'ga-ga-ga'
Habitat Beaches, farmland,
rubbish tips, cliffs
Breeding 2–3 eggs are
laid in May

SUPER FACT

Herring gulls are omnivores. This means that they can eat a wide range of food. They often follow fishing boats for miles, waiting for fish scraps to be thrown overboard.

PHOTO FILE

Herring gulls have bright yellow bills and an obvious red spot on the lower bill. They fly by soaring and gliding on the wind.

MY NOTES & PICTURES

I'VE SEEN IT... Eating ◯ Flying ◯ Nesting ◯

HERRING GULL *Larus argentatus*

The most widespread of all British coastal birds, the herring gull is well known to holidaymakers at seaside towns and beaches. These large birds have little fear of humans and will approach them for food. They also have other ways of feeding, such as trampling on mud to make worms come to the surface and scouring rubbish tips looking for morsels to eat. Herring gulls have even been seen to drop crabs and other shellfish on rocks or roads to break them open.

SCALE

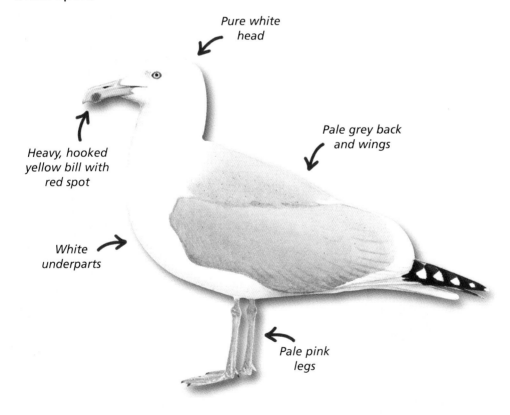

Pure white head

Pale grey back and wings

Heavy, hooked yellow bill with red spot

White underparts

Pale pink legs

BIRDS

FACT FILE

Size 34–39 cm
Wingspan 65–80 cm
Call 'Kee-eee'
Habitat Woodlands, farms, heaths
Breeding 4–6 eggs are laid from March–June

SUPER FACT

Kestrels were once common in British farms, but their numbers are in decline. This is probably due to the loss of their habitats, which has meant a shortage of food.

PHOTO FILE

Kestrels spread their fan-shaped tails when they want to slow down, especially when they are planning to swoop on their prey.

MY NOTES & PICTURES

I'VE SEEN IT... Eating ◯   Flying ◯   Nesting ◯

KESTREL *Falco tinnunculus*

Native birds of prey, kestrels are often spotted hovering above roadside verges. They perch on telegraph poles or tall trees nearby, looking out for opportunities to feed on prey, such as small mammals (especially voles), beetles, worms and small birds. Kestrels have extraordinary eyesight and can spot a beetle 50 metres away. If they catch a number of voles in one day, they may hide the leftovers and eat them later on – usually as the sun is setting.

SCALE

Short, round head

Back is spotted with black

Slim tail with a black band

FACT FILE

Size 16–17 cm
Wingspan 24–26 cm
Call Loud and sharp 'kit-chee'
Habitat Rivers, canals, coasts
Breeding There are two broods a year, in May and July, and 5–7 eggs are laid

SUPER FACT

Kingfishers have their own territories, or hunting grounds. A territory may be a 1–5 km stretch of water that the bird has to defend.

PHOTO FILE

Males and females look similar, but the males have bolder colours and their bills are all black. Females have red marks on their bills.

MY NOTES & PICTURES

I'VE SEEN IT... Eating ◯ Flying ◯ Nesting ◯

KINGFISHER *Alcedo atthis*

Kingfishers live near slow-moving shallow waterways, where they can hunt for small fish, especially minnows and sticklebacks. They favour places with trees that overhang the water, as they provide perfect perching posts where the birds can wait patiently, watching for prey. As it dives into the water, a kingfisher opens its bill, closes its eyes and catches the fish. It returns to the perch, where it kills the fish by smashing it against the branch. One bird must eat its bodyweight in fish every day.

SCALE

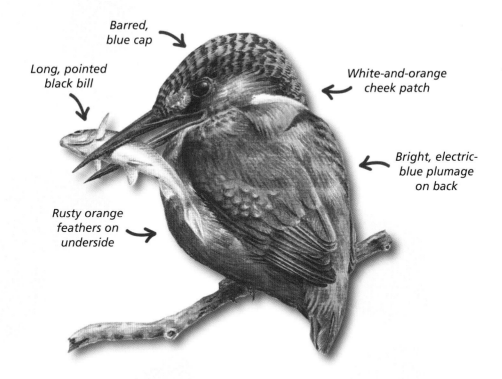

Barred, blue cap

Long, pointed black bill

White-and-orange cheek patch

Bright, electric-blue plumage on back

Rusty orange feathers on underside

BIRDS

FACT FILE

Size 28–31 cm
Wingspan 70–76 cm
Call 'weet' or 'whee-er-ee'
Habitat Fields, farmland, wet moors, near rivers
Breeding 3–4 eggs are laid from March–April and the young hatch 3–4 weeks later

SUPER FACT

Lapwings make their nests in hollows on the ground. They choose places where they have a good all-round view, so they can spot predators.

PHOTO FILE

Male lapwings have long crests and the feathers on their back are dark green, with patches of purple and copper.

MY NOTES & PICTURES

I'VE SEEN IT... Eating ◯   Flying ◯   Nesting ◯

LAPWING   *Vanellus vanellus*

Once widespread on farms, lapwings are
becoming less common because of
modern farming techniques. Their black-and-
white plumage, striking crest and unusual
wavering flight pattern make lapwings easy to
identify. They often survive the winters living
in large flocks, but the birds separate in spring
to go to their breeding grounds. At this time,
the males start to display to females by rolling,
diving and zigzagging in flight.

SCALE

*Dark green
plumage
on back*

*Black cap
with crest*

*Short,
dark bill*

*White
underwing*

AT THE...   Farm ◯   River ◯   Lake ◯

BIRDS

FACT FILE

Size 26–28 cm

Wingspan 42–48 cm

Call Loud rattling chatter 'tsarrk' or flute-like song

Habitat Parks, farms, gardens

Breeding 3–5 eggs are laid and there are two broods a year, from March–June

SUPER FACT

Mistle thrushes are usually shy of people, but they have been known to attack other animals, even dogs, during their breeding season.

PHOTO FILE

Mistle thrushes perch high in trees and draw attention to themselves with their loud, powerful calls and songs.

MY NOTES & PICTURES

I'VE SEEN IT... Eating ◯　　Flying ◯　　Nesting ◯

MISTLE THRUSH *Turdus viscivorus*

The **mistle thrush is Britain's largest thrush.** It is also known as the 'stormcock', because it sings in the treetops when the wind is blowing hard. It forages on the ground for insects, worms and snails in spring and summer and moves by bounding along in leaps. In the winter, mistle thrushes feed on fruit and berries, especially yew, hawthorn, holly, mistletoe and ivy. These birds are common across the whole of Britain, except the northern and western isles of Scotland.

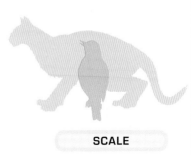

SCALE

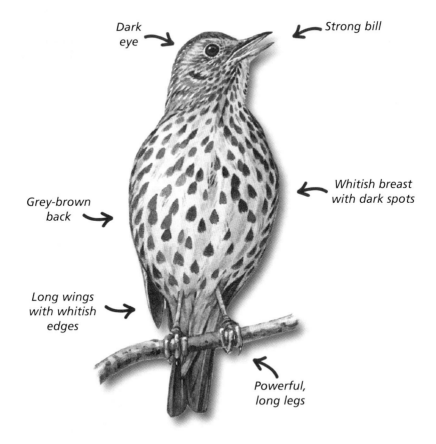

Dark eye

Strong bill

Whitish breast with dark spots

Grey-brown back

Long wings with whitish edges

Powerful, long legs

FACT FILE

Size 1.4–1.6 m
Wingspan 2–2.35 m
Call Loud trumpet or hiss
Habitat Lakes, rivers, marshes
Breeding Up to eight eggs
may be laid anytime
from March–June

SUPER FACT

Swans were once regarded as valuable birds and were traded between noblemen. Today, the Queen owns British mute swans and still employs a Swan Keeper.

PHOTO FILE

When cygnets hatch they have brown-grey plumage and grey bills. As the birds grow, patches of white feathers begin to appear.

MY NOTES & PICTURES

I'VE SEEN IT... Eating ○ Flying ○ Nesting ○

MUTE SWAN *Cygnus olor*

There are three types of swan that can be seen in Britain – mute, Bewick's and whooper. Mute swans are the only ones that are resident all year round. These large waterbirds mate for life. The male is called a cob, the female is a pen and the young are called cygnets. Both parents incubate the eggs and, once hatched, the cygnets sometimes ride around on their parents' backs. Mute swans mostly eat vegetation from the riverbed, which they can reach with their long necks.

SCALE

Large black swelling at base of bill

Long, elegant, curved neck

Adult plumage is all white (but brown in cygnets)

Orange-red bill

BIRDS

FACT FILE

Size 16–17 cm
Wingspan 23–26 cm
Call Very varied fast song
Habitat Thickets, bushes, dense woodlands
Breeding 4–5 eggs are laid in a single brood from May–June

SUPER FACT

Legend states nightingales sing all night to stay awake. They are meant to have stolen an eye from a slow worm, which spends the nights trying to get it back.

PHOTO FILE

Although secretive and difficult to see, nightingales can be heard singing, both day and night, from April until early June.

MY NOTES & PICTURES

I'VE SEEN IT... Eating ◯ Flying ◯ Nesting ◯

NIGHTINGALE *Luscinia megarhynchos*

The nightingale is known for its beautiful, melodic song, which has a huge range of high and low notes that few other birds can match. Males are heard singing after dark, but they do sing during the daytime too. Nightingales are difficult to spot because they have dull plumage and prefer to live in places with lots of vegetation, where they can hide. Nightingales are summer visitors to Britain and are not often seen outside the southeast of England. They feed on beetles, larvae, berries and worms.

SCALE

Pale ring around the eye

Red-brown upper feathers

Long, reddish tail

White throat and underbelly

Pinkish legs

BIRDS

FACT FILE

Size 11–15 cm
Wingspan 20–25 cm
Call Loud piping notes
Habitat Woodlands, parks, gardens
Breeding 6–9 white eggs, from April–May

SUPER FACT

Nuthatches are easily mistaken for woodpeckers, as they both perch on the bark of trees. Nuthatches, however, are the only birds that run headfirst down a tree.

PHOTO FILE

Nuthatches visit bird tables and seed feeders. They wedge nuts into cracks in trees and hammer them open with their beaks.

MY NOTES & PICTURES

I'VE SEEN IT... Eating ◯ Flying ◯ Nesting ◯

NUTHATCH *Sitta europaea*

U nusual looking birds, nuthatches are often seen running up and down the trunks of trees, searching for insects. They use their sharp, pointed beaks to search cracks in tree bark for bugs or seeds. Males and females look similar, but the colours are slightly darker in males. They live in woodlands, but often visit gardens in search of nuts and seeds.

SCALE

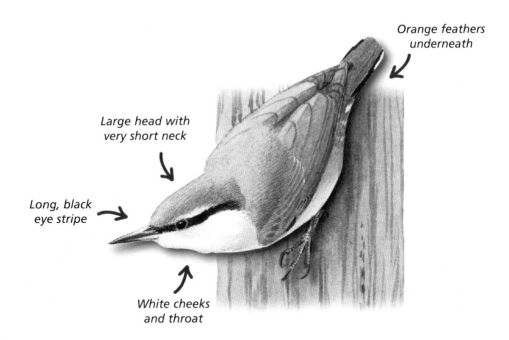

Orange feathers underneath

Large head with very short neck

Long, black eye stripe

White cheeks and throat

FACT FILE

Size 40–45 cm
Wingspan 80–85 cm
Call Loud 'kleep kleep'
Habitat Beaches, islands,
river valleys
Breeding 2–3 eggs are
laid from April–July

SUPER FACT

Oystercatchers compete with
fishermen for clams and mussels.
In the 1970s, thousands of these
birds were killed so the fishermen
could take the shellfish instead.

PHOTO FILE

Bright, bold and noisy, oystercatchers are
easy to identify. They build nests in scrapes
of sand or shingle near the water's edge.

MY NOTES & PICTURES

I'VE SEEN IT... Eating ◯ Flying ◯ Nesting ◯

OYSTERCATCHER

Haematopus ostralegus

The oystercatcher has a strong bill that it uses to break open shellfish, such as cockles and mussels. These distinctive, sturdy birds live in most British coastal regions throughout the year, and often form enormous flocks that make a raucous noise. They walk along the seashore or mudflats, head down, as they search for food to eat. When they live inland, oystercatchers rely on earthworms as a major source of food. Despite their name, oystercatchers do not appear to eat oysters.

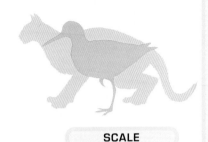

SCALE

Black-and-white plumage

Bright red eye

Long, bright orange bill

Large, bulky body

White wing bands

Pale pink legs

BIRDS

FACT FILE

Size 39–50 cm

Wingspan 1–1.2 m

Call 'kee-kee' or 'hak-kaak'

Habitat Open ground, hills, coasts, cliffs

Breeding 2–4 eggs are laid in a single brood from March–June

SUPER FACT

By the 1960s, 80 percent of the British peregrine population had died due to pesticide poisoning. The worst pesticides were banned and populations have grown.

PHOTO FILE

Peregrine falcons have eyes that face forwards rather than to the side. This helps them focus on their prey when they hunt.

MY NOTES & PICTURES

I'VE SEEN IT... Eating ◯ Flying ◯ Nesting ◯

PEREGRINE FALCON   *Falco peregrinus*

Peregrine falcons are birds of prey that live **throughout Europe.** They can adapt to a wide range of habitats, as long as there is enough food to support them. Peregrines mostly feed on other birds, such as pigeons, which they catch in flight. They can see their prey at a great distance, then swoop in for the kill, reaching top speeds of 180 km/h. Once they have caught their prey, peregrines eat almost the entire body, leaving just the intestines and the breastbone.

SCALE

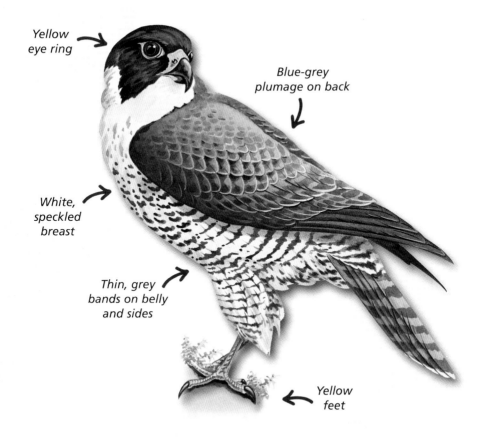

Yellow eye ring

Blue-grey plumage on back

White, speckled breast

Thin, grey bands on belly and sides

Yellow feet

BIRDS

FACT FILE

Size 26–29 cm

Wingspan 47–63 cm

Call Loud 'aar' or 'kar-ooo-ar'

Habitat Cliffs, offshore islands

Breeding One egg is laid from May–June and the adults stay in the breeding area until August

SUPER FACT

When young puffins leave the nest they head for the sea, following the light. Sometimes they are confused by nearby city bright lights, and head inland instead.

PHOTO FILE

Puffins live in flocks and lay their eggs in burrows or caves. In winter, their bills lose their bold colours and become dark and dull.

MY NOTES & PICTURES

I'VE SEEN IT... Eating ◯ Flying ◯ Nesting ◯

PUFFIN *Fratercula arctica*

The puffin is an unmistakeable sea bird with its black crown, colourful summer bill and clown-like white face. Puffins breed in large colonies in Britain and Ireland. They are skilled divers, and can swim to depths of 15 metres to catch several fish at a time without surfacing. They build their nests in burrows that they dig themselves, or they use old rabbit burrows. Puffins have large, strong feet that they use as air-brakes when landing, as well as for swimming and digging.

SCALE

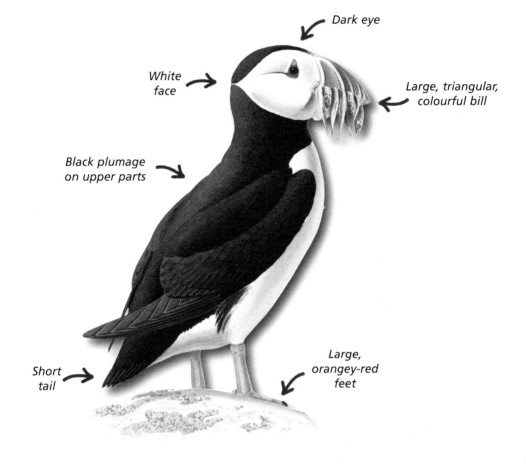

Dark eye

White face

Large, triangular, colourful bill

Black plumage on upper parts

Short tail

Large, orangey-red feet

BIRDS

FACT FILE

Size 20–22 cm

Wingspan 33–35 cm

Call Variable songs from 'seep' to 'chuk'

Habitat Woods, heaths, farms, parks, gardens

Breeding 4–6 eggs are laid in each two broods from April–July

SUPER FACT

Redwings travel far and wide to search for food, but they are very vulnerable to cold and a shortage of food. If there are no berries, they may die in their hundreds.

PHOTO FILE

In cold weather, redwings often struggle to find food, so they may start foraging on the ground, searching for fallen fruit and berries.

MY NOTES & PICTURES

I'VE SEEN IT... Eating ○ Flying ○ Nesting ○

REDWING *Turdus iliacus*

Unlike garden thrushes, redwings are most commonly seen in woods and fields, often in large flocks. They forage for worms, slugs, snails, insects and berries, sometimes in the company of fieldfares and song thrushes. Large groups may settle on one tree and stay there until they have stripped all its berries. These birds are winter visitors to Britain, many of them travelling here from Scandinavia. They return to the continent in March, ready for the breeding season.

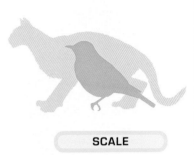

SCALE

Dark cap

Bold white eye-stripe

Silver-white feathers on underside with speckles

Chesnut-red flanks

BIRDS

FACT FILE

Size 12–15 cm
Wingspan 20–22 cm
Call Warbling song
Habitat Gardens, parks, woodlands
Breeding 5–6 white eggs, speckled with red, from March–July

SUPER FACT

Robins do not migrate from the UK, but in winter, robins from colder countries often migrate to the UK. They have paler breasts and are less tame.

PHOTO FILE

Juvenile (young) robins do not have red breasts. It is thought that this stops adults fighting with them for territory or food.

MY NOTES & PICTURES

I'VE SEEN IT... Eating ◯ Flying ◯ Nesting ◯

ROBIN   *Erithacus rubecula*

One of the most easily recognized garden birds, robins are dainty, with plump bodies and red breasts. The back is brown and the underneath is white. They are known as gardeners' friends as they often perch nearby when soil is being dug over, and they quickly leap on any insects that are exposed. Males and females look similar. Robins are associated with holly berries, not only because of Christmas, but also because in winter, when food is scarce, robins feed on the berries.

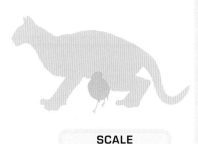

SCALE

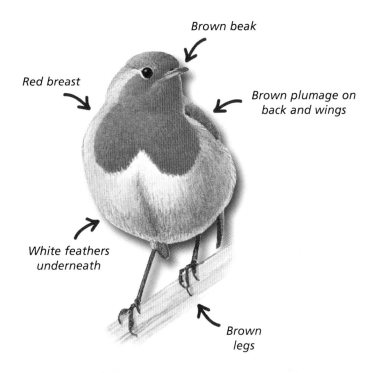

Brown beak

Red breast

Brown plumage on back and wings

White feathers underneath

Brown legs

IN THE... Garden   Park   Countryside

FACT FILE

Size 44–46 cm
Wingspan 81–99 cm
Call Very loud raucous 'caaar'
Habitat Farms, parks, gardens
Breeding 3–6 eggs are laid
from March–June

SUPER FACT

There are more than a million
breeding pairs of rooks in
Britain. However, numbers
dropped drastically in the 1960s
because of pesticide poisoning.

PHOTO FILE

Rooks live in groups, and when a large
number of them start calling and cawing
the noise can become unbearably loud.

MY NOTES & PICTURES

I'VE SEEN IT... Eating ◯   Flying ◯   Nesting ◯

ROOK *Corvus frugilegus*

The rook is one of the best-known British social birds, which lives in large flocks or colonies that are sometimes called 'parliaments'. They often build their nests close to one another, and in the winter, the tops of trees may be home to a number of these birds and their large nests. Rooks fly with a slow, flapping and gliding flight pattern. They feed on caterpillars, snails, larvae and grain, but may gather near roadsides to feed on animals that have been killed by vehicles.

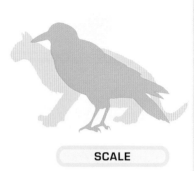

SCALE

Long, thin, grey bill

Black, glossy plumage

Bare face

Ragged-looking breast and leg feathers

FACT FILE

Size 11–13 cm
Wingspan 20–23 cm
Call Clear 'tsu-ee' or rapid trills
Habitat Conifer forests,
gardens, near rivers
Breeding 4–5 eggs are laid
in one or two broods
from May–July

SUPER FACT

Siskins love seeds, but they will visit gardens where they can find regular supplies of shelled peanuts. They also love the seeds of alder and birch trees.

PHOTO FILE

Female siskins have paler grey heads than the males, and there are distinctive black streaks on the white belly feathers.

MY NOTES & PICTURES

I'VE SEEN IT... Eating ◯ Flying ◯ Nesting ◯

SISKIN *Carduelis spinus*

Siskins are commonly found in conifer **woods.** Their numbers have grown in recent years because of the increase of conifer plantations around Britain. They have spread further south and can now be found all across the country throughout the year. During the winter, siskins often gather in large flocks, sometimes in the company of redpolls, which are a type of small finch. In spring, the males sometimes perch at the top of trees so their songs can carry further.

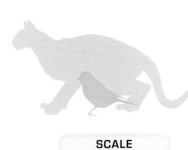

SCALE

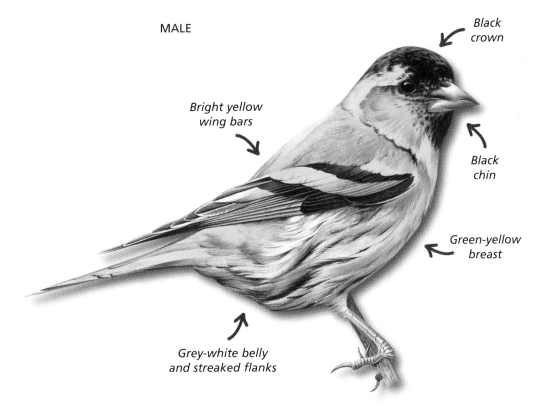

MALE

Black crown

Bright yellow wing bars

Black chin

Green-yellow breast

Grey-white belly and streaked flanks

FACT FILE

Size 28–40 cm

Wingspan 60–80 cm

Call 'kekek' followed by 'peee'

Habitat Woods, farmland, marshes, gardens

Breeding 4–5 eggs are laid in one brood from March–June

SUPER FACT

Sparrowhawks fly at speeds of up to 50 km/h and need to get close to their prey before reaching out with their powerful talons.

PHOTO FILE

Sparrowhawks grasp their prey with powerful talons, or claws, and rip at the flesh with their sharp bill. They usually eat other birds.

MY NOTES & PICTURES

SPARROWHAWK *Accipiter nisus*

Sparrowhawks are native residents, and are becoming more common around Britain following a severe drop in numbers caused by pesticide poisoning. The female is larger than the male, has brown upperparts and a white stripe over the eye. These birds of prey have rounded wings and long tails that are perfect for fast flight and weaving in and out of trees. Sparrowhawks do not hover. Many chicks fail to survive winter because of a lack of food and few sparrowhawks live for more than three years.

SCALE

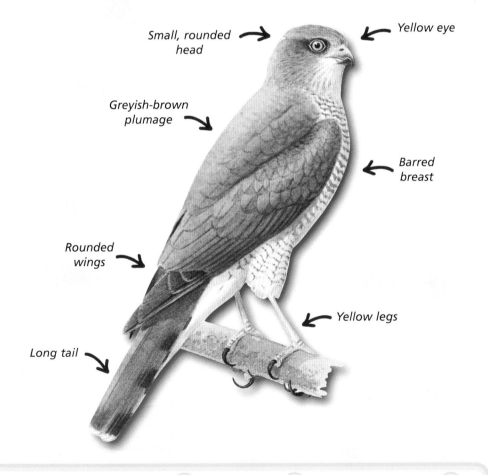

Small, rounded head

Yellow eye

Greyish-brown plumage

Barred breast

Rounded wings

Yellow legs

Long tail

BIRDS

FACT FILE

Size 16–17 cm

Wingspan 42–48 cm

Call Loud screeches and screams

Habitat Open areas, towns, cities

Breeding 2–3 eggs are laid from May–June

SUPER FACT

British swifts spend the winter in Africa, where they follow the rains. After rainfall, insect populations boom, providing a good food supply for these birds.

PHOTO FILE

Swifts line their nests with feathers that help to keep the eggs warm. If eggs lose too much heat, the chicks growing inside them will die.

MY NOTES & PICTURES

I'VE SEEN IT... Eating ◯   Flying ◯   Nesting ◯

SWIFT *Apus apus*

Swifts are extraordinary birds and superb **fliers.** They rarely come to land and spend almost all of their lives in the air, even sleeping while in flight. Once fledglings leave the nest they may remain airborne for the next two or three years, until they reach breeding age. Swifts feed on insects and spiders that they catch in mid-air. They arrive in Britain in April, for the breeding season, and often nest in the eaves of old buildings. They leave in July or August.

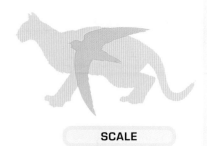

SCALE

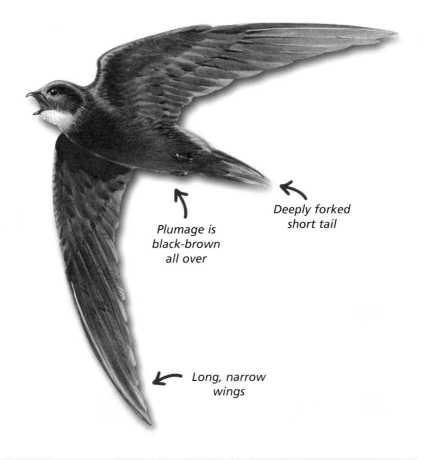

Plumage is black-brown all over

Deeply forked short tail

Long, narrow wings

FACT FILE

Size 37–39 cm

Wingspan 94–104 cm

Call Hooting 'hoo-hoo' or 'ke-wik'

Habitat Woodland, farmland, gardens

Breeding 2–5 eggs are laid in a single brood from April–June

SUPER FACT

Tawny owls can look behind by twisting their heads round. They can pinpoint sound accurately by moving their heads to get a 'fix' on the source of the noise.

PHOTO FILE

The heart-shaped face of this tawny owl helps to direct sound towards its ears, which are hidden beneath the thick, fluffy plumage.

MY NOTES & PICTURES

I'VE SEEN IT... Eating ◯ Flying ◯ Nesting ◯

TAWNY OWL *Strix aluco*

The tawny owl is a woodland predator that also lives in parks and gardens. These nocturnal birds normally hunt for small mammals, but they have moved into urban areas in search of small birds that are gathered around a bird table. Like other owls, these birds fly in eerie silence, their wing-beats muffled by the downy edges of their wing feathers. As well as mammals and birds, tawny owls also feed on insects, newts, frogs and bats.

SCALE

Mottled, brown feathers

Large round head with distinctive facial disc and dark eyes

Paler colouring on underside

FACT FILE

Size 34–38 cm

Wingspan 58–64 cm

Call Female: 'quack', male: 'crik-crik'

Habitat Wetlands, estuaries

Breeding 8–11 eggs are laid from April–June

SUPER FACT

Male teals, called drakes, may put on displays of head-bobbing to impress a female. These displays help females choose the best and healthiest mates.

PHOTO FILE

These nervous birds often fly near to water, swooping and darting over the surface several times before they attempt to land.

MY NOTES & PICTURES

I'VE SEEN IT... Eating ◯ Flying ◯ Nesting ◯

TEAL *Anas crecca*

Many of the teals in Britain stay here all **year round.** However, a number of them travel here from Siberia and north-west Europe to spend the winters, especially in central and western areas. These are the smallest British surface-feeding ducks, and they often live together in groups ranging in size from 20 to several hundred. These small ducks are quick and agile, and move easily around the edges of the water, searching for vegetation to eat.

SCALE

MALE

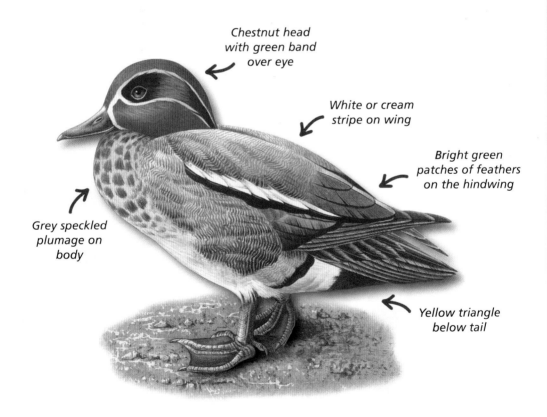

Chestnut head with green band over eye

White or cream stripe on wing

Bright green patches of feathers on the hindwing

Grey speckled plumage on body

Yellow triangle below tail

BIRDS

FACT FILE

Size 15–17 cm
Wingspan 23–29 cm
Call quick 'tsik' or trilling 'ti-ti-ti'
Habitat Fields, farms, heaths, grasslands
Breeding 3–5 eggs are laid with up to three broods every year

SUPER FACT

The yellowhammer's song is sometimes described as sounding like 'a little bit of bread and no cheese'. With a little imagination, it is a good description!

PHOTO FILE

This male yellowhammer has a distinctive yellow face. The females have darker backs and dark streaks on their faces and bellies.

MY NOTES & PICTURES

I'VE SEEN IT... Eating ◯   Flying ◯   Nesting ◯

YELLOWHAMMER

Emberiza citrinella

Small flocks of yellowhammers used to be a common sight on hedgerows, feeding on seeds or perched on telegraph wires singing all day long. Sadly, their numbers have declined drastically in recent years, making the British population of these pretty songbirds at risk. The most likely reason for this is the loss of habitat, which has reduced their food supply. These birds are native and live in all regions of Britain.

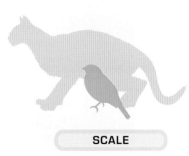

SCALE

MALE

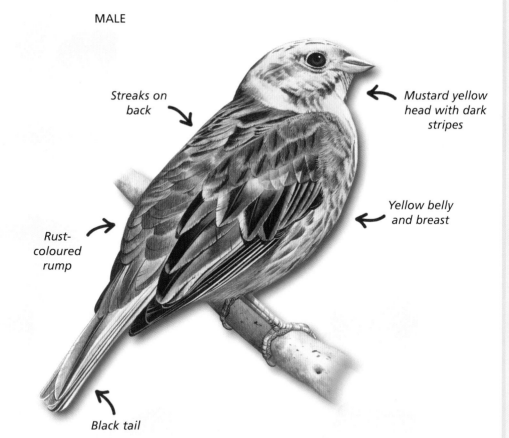

Streaks on back

Mustard yellow head with dark stripes

Yellow belly and breast

Rust-coloured rump

Black tail

FACT FILE

Size 50–90 cm

Habitat Heaths, grassland, woods, moors

Hibernation September or October–March

Breeding 3–18 young born in August or September

SUPER FACT

Most reptiles lay eggs, but adders are viviparous snakes, which means they keep the eggs inside their bodies while they develop and give birth to live young.

PHOTO FILE

Snakes, like this adder, learn about the world around them using their excellent senses of sight, sound, smell and taste.

MY NOTES & PICTURES

I'VE SEEN A... Juvenile   Adult ◯

ADDER *Vipera berus*

Adders are Britain's only venomous snakes. However, they are so secretive and non-aggressive that they do not pose any real danger to humans. These reptiles are found throughout Britain and are widespread in Scotland and parts of southern England. Adders are active in the day, and in warm weather they may be seen hunting for small animals, such as birds, lizards and frogs. They bite their prey with fangs, which inject venom, or poison, straight into the victim's flesh.

SCALE

MALE

Border of spots near zigzag

Vertical pupil

Dark zigzag pattern on the back

Males are grey, white or cream but females are red-brown

IN THE... Garden ◯ Park ◯ Countryside ◯

FACT FILE

Size 6–8 cm

Habitat Shady, damp places

Hibernation November–February

Breeding Mating in spring
and the eggs are laid
in still water

SUPER FACT

Frogs have long, sticky tongues
that they shoot out to catch flies
and other insects. Frogs are friends
to gardeners as they also eat
pests, such as snails and slugs.

PHOTO FILE

Adult frogs have smooth skin and long
hind legs. The colour and pattern of their
skin varies, but most are greenish brown.

MY NOTES & PICTURES

I'VE SEEN A... Juvenile ◯   Adult ◯

COMMON FROG *Rana temporaria*

Found in moist, shady habitats, common frogs often live in ponds, lakes or rivers. Adult frogs come together in spring to lay their eggs in water. One female can lay up to 2000 eggs, called spawn, in a clump. Young, or juvenile, frogs are called tadpoles. They live in water until they change into adults. They can survive cold winter months by sleeping in mud at the bottom of a pond.

SCALE

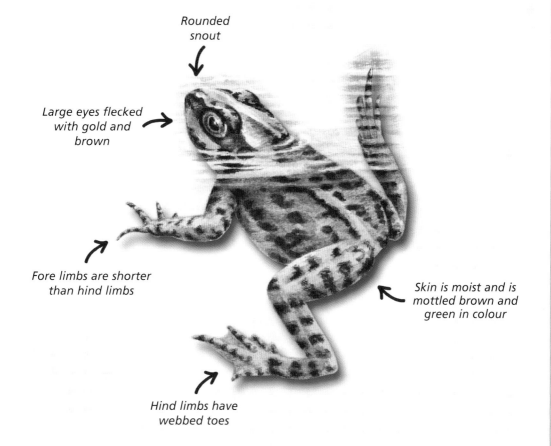

Rounded snout

Large eyes flecked with gold and brown

Fore limbs are shorter than hind limbs

Skin is moist and is mottled brown and green in colour

Hind limbs have webbed toes

FACT FILE

Size 5–9 cm

Habitat Watery or wet gardens, woods

Hibernation Late autumn– early spring

Breeding From March–June and 1000–3000 eggs are laid

SUPER FACT

Toad skin is a useful organ that can change colour to suit the animal's surroundings, and even produce toxins to deter predators.

PHOTO FILE

Toads are amphibians and can take in oxygen from the air, or through their moist, warty skin. They prefer wet habitats.

MY NOTES & PICTURES

I'VE SEEN A... Juvenile ◯ Adult ◯

COMMON TOAD *Bufo bufo*

Common toads are found all over Britain, **except northern Scotland, in damp or wet places.** These amphibians are mostly nocturnal and eat a range of prey including spiders, worms, snails and slugs. Adults travel to pools or ponds in the autumn and as the cold weather draws in, they hibernate in leaf piles or burrows. In the spring they mate, and males gather around the females in large groups. The females lay their eggs in water, which then develop into tadpoles.

SCALE

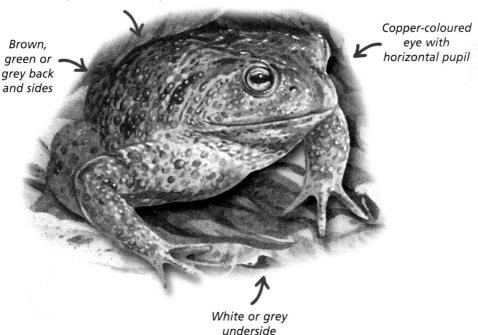

Warty skin that produces toxins (poisons)

Brown, green or grey back and sides

Copper-coloured eye with horizontal pupil

White or grey underside

IN THE... Garden ◯ Park ◯ Countryside ◯

FACT FILE

Size 1.2–2 m

Habitat Low-growing vegetation

Hibernation October–March

Breeding Mating in March and April

SUPER FACT

If grass snakes are disturbed, they dive into water and hide amongst the weeds. They are excellent swimmers and can stay underwater for up to one hour.

PHOTO FILE

In summer, females lay 8–40 eggs, often in compost heaps, rotting logs or leaf litter. The young look like adults, but smaller.

MY NOTES & PICTURES

I'VE SEEN A... Juvenile ◯   Adult ◯

GRASS SNAKE *Natrix natrix*

Shy animals, it is rare to see grass snakes even if they are present. Females are usually longer than males, and can reach up to 2 m in length. Grass snakes feed on a variety of animals, including mice, frogs, tadpoles, newts, fish and birds. They are excellent swimmers and spend much of their time in ponds and slow-moving waters.

SCALE

Slender body

Greyish-green
scaly skin

Pale banding
behind head

Dark marks along
flanks of body

Pale
underside

REPTILES & AMPHIBIANS

FACT FILE

Size 11–16 cm

Habitat Near pools and ponds

Hibernation October–February

Breeding Mating in March and April and the eggs are laid in water

PHOTO FILE

Great crested newts spend the day hiding among vegetation, in burrows or under rocks. This is a female newt – she has no crest.

SUPER FACT

The tadpoles of the great crested newt look like adults, only smaller, when their legs have formed. They stay in water for four months before they can breathe air.

MY NOTES & PICTURES

I'VE SEEN A... Juvenile ◯ Adult ◯

GREAT CRESTED NEWT *Triturus cristatus*

Easily recognized by their colourful bodies, which are covered in warty bumps, great crested newts are large amphibians. The upper body is usually muddy brown, grey or black, and the underside is bright orange or yellow, and covered in black marks. Males have a long crest on their back and a tail that grows bigger during the breeding season. These newts prefer moist habitats, such as ponds, to dry places, but they are able to travel a short distance from water.

SCALE

MALE

Long, jagged crest (in males only)

Small head and eyes

Orange skin with black marks

Dark brown skin, covered in warty bumps

White or blue streak on tail

FACT FILE

Size Up to 40 cm

Habitat Gardens, farms, parks, woods

Hibernation October–March

Breeding Mating occurs once in two years and eight live young are born August–September

SUPER FACT

Slow worms favour compost heaps, where they can find food in the form of small invertebrates. They can also keep warm in the rotting vegetation, which gives off heat.

PHOTO FILE

Slow worms have smooth skin that looks wet, but is actually dry. Like other reptiles, they sometimes bask in the sun to get warm.

MY NOTES & PICTURES

I'VE SEEN A... Juvenile Adult ◯

SLOW WORM
Anguis fragilis

Despite their snake-like appearance, slow worms are actually limbless lizards. These reptiles are found throughout Britain, especially in southern regions and in gardens where they eat many pests. Their Latin name means 'fragile snake', which reflects the fact that they can easily drop their tails if attacked. The tail continues to wriggle, distracting the predator while the lizard escapes. A new tail begins to grow in just two weeks. Slow worms can live for many years, with one having lived to over 50.

SCALE

FEMALE

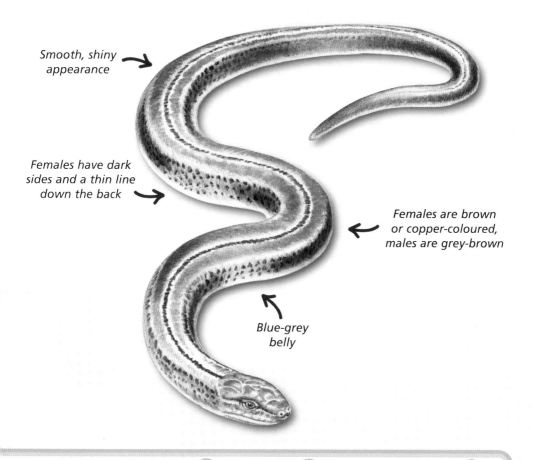

Smooth, shiny appearance

Females have dark sides and a thin line down the back

Females are brown or copper-coloured, males are grey-brown

Blue-grey belly

IN THE... Garden ⬤ Park ⬤ Countryside ⬤

REPTILES & AMPHIBIANS

FACT FILE

Size 10–15 cm
Habitat Open areas
Hibernation October–March
Breeding Mating in spring
and young are born from
June onwards

SUPER FACT

Most reptiles lay eggs. However,
viviparous lizards keep their eggs
inside their bodies until they are
ready to hatch. Between three
and 20 eggs hatch in a litter.

PHOTO FILE

Viviparous lizards have good senses of sight
and smell. They pounce on their prey, shake
it to stun it, then swallow it whole.

MY NOTES & PICTURES

I'VE SEEN A... Juvenile ◯   Adult ◯

VIVIPAROUS LIZARD *Lacerta vivipara*

Lizards are reptiles and, unlike newts, can spend all their lives on land. Their skin is dry and scaly, and they often bask in the sun to warm their bodies. The viviparous lizard is also known as the common lizard. It has short legs and a very long tail, which may be twice the length of the body. The colours and patterns vary, but most are mixed shades of green and brown. Males are darker than females. These lizards are good swimmers.

SCALE

MALE

Dark line down the back and white markings

Limbs positioned on sides of body

Males have a pinky-orange belly

Tail may be twice the length of the body

Dry, rough, scaly skin

FISH

FACT FILE

Size Up to 30 cm

Habitat From small brooks to large rivers and lakes

Found Widespread

Breeding Spawning occurs in the winter and eggs take 3–4 months to develop and hatch

SUPER FACT

Like some other fish, trout eggs and young fish (larvae) can take a long time to mature into adults – up to four years. They develop more slowly in cold water.

PHOTO FILE

It is rare to see a trout clearly in water, because they prefer to swim in vegetation or below rocks. They have long, powerful bodies.

MY NOTES & PICTURES

I'VE SEEN A... Juvenile  Adult

BROWN TROUT *Salmo trutta*

It is difficult to identify brown trout because their appearance can vary enormously, depending on where they live. Some are dull with deep colours, while others are bright and speckled. They can also be difficult to spot because these large fish like to hide beneath cover, and are most likely to be found resting along riverbanks or under bridges. Trout are predators, and have rows of sharp teeth in their large mouths. They eat insects, worms and crustaceans.

SCALE

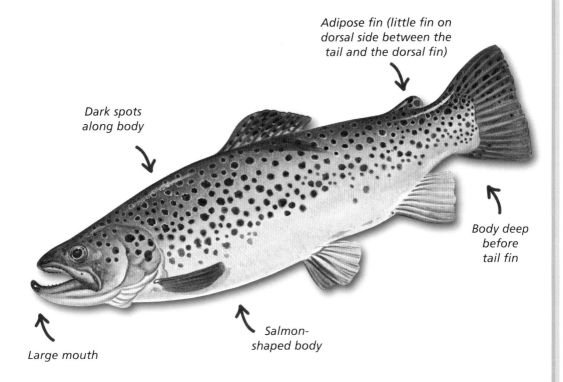

Adipose fin (little fin on dorsal side between the tail and the dorsal fin)

Dark spots along body

Body deep before tail fin

Large mouth

Salmon-shaped body

IN THE...   Stream ◯   River ◯   Lake ◯

FISH

FACT FILE

Size Up to 1.2 m

Habitat Slow-moving or still freshwater

Found Widespread

Breeding Spawning occurs in the summer and females can lay up to one million eggs a season

SUPER FACT

There are different types of common carp, including leather carp, with no scales, king carp and mirror carp, with a single row of shiny scales on the sides.

PHOTO FILE

There are fleshy growths on either side of a carp's mouth. These growths, called barbels, are very sensitive and help the fish find food.

MY NOTES & PICTURES

I'VE SEEN A... Juvenile Adult

COMMON CARP *Cyprinus carpio*

Carp were first introduced to Britain in the 1300s, possibly from the river Danube in Europe, where a wild population still exists. They have been bred for centuries and have often been kept in ponds as ornamental fish. Now they are found in many bodies of water and they are common throughout Britain. These freshwater fish eat plants and small animals that they find in the muddy sediment at the bottom of ponds.

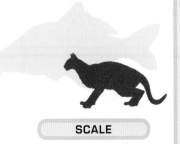

SCALE

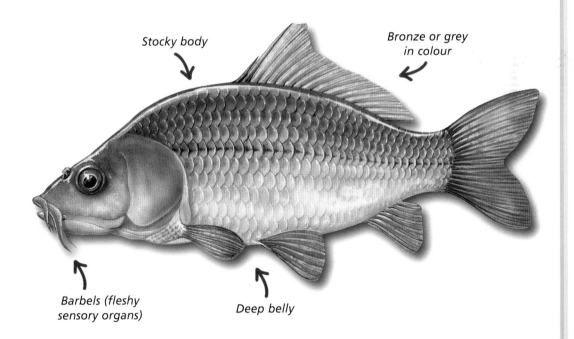

Stocky body

Bronze or grey in colour

Barbels (fleshy sensory organs)

Deep belly

IN THE...   Pond ◯   Lake ◯   River ◯

FISH

FACT FILE

Size 6–10 cm

Habitat Clean streams or rivers

Found Widespread

Breeding Spawning occurs from April–June and adults migrate upstream to reach their spawning areas

SUPER FACT

Minnows are an important source of food for many other animals that share their habitat. Kingfishers, herons, otters and larger fish all prey upon them.

PHOTO FILE

Minnows are closely related to carp and like them can feed on a wide range of food. This minnow is eating a worm.

MY NOTES & PICTURES

I'VE SEEN A... Juvenile 　　　　Adult

MINNOW *Phoxinus phoxinus*

Minnows live in large groups, or shoals, and are most commonly found in bodies of water that are clean and contain plenty of oxygen. They live throughout Britain, except northern Scotland. These small fish feed on plants, algae, insects, molluscs and crustaceans. In the springtime they swim to shallow, pebbled stretches of river where they mate and lay their eggs. At this time the males change appearance, becoming brighter and developing different colours to the females.

SCALE

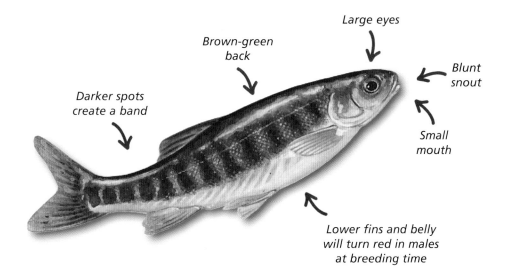

Large eyes

Brown-green back

Blunt snout

Darker spots create a band

Small mouth

Lower fins and belly will turn red in males at breeding time

FACT FILE

Size 10–25 cm

Habitat Freshwater lakes, canals, slow-moving rivers

Found Widespread

Breeding Spawning occurs from April–June and up to 100,000 eggs are laid at a time

SUPER FACT

Roach are able to live in dirty water, and water with some salt (which is described as 'brackish'). They are able to cope with most conditions and many habitats.

PHOTO FILE

Like other bony fish, roach are covered in scales. As scales grow they make 'growth lines', which can be counted to give the animal's age.

MY NOTES & PICTURES

I'VE SEEN A... Juvenile ◯ Adult ◯

ROACH *Rutilus rutilus*

Common freshwater fish, roach are **widespread throughout all of Europe.** It is easiest to spot them in the spring, when they become very active around breeding time. They mostly eat insect larvae and small molluscs, but roach themselves are eaten by herons, pikes, eels, mink and some birds of prey. These fish are also caught by anglers in large numbers. Roach are slow-growing and do not reach maturity until two to three years of age.

SCALE

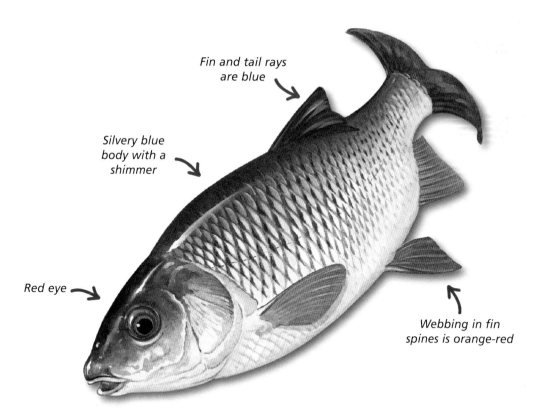

Fin and tail rays are blue

Silvery blue body with a shimmer

Red eye

Webbing in fin spines is orange-red

IN THE... Lake ◯ Canal ◯ River ◯

FISH

FACT FILE

Size Up to 1.5 m

Habitat Open ocean, clean rivers

Found Scotland and some scattered rivers elsewhere

Breeding Spawning occurs in November, in the salmons' birthplace

SUPER FACT

Until the 19th century, people thought that young salmon were a completely different species from the adults, and no one understood their complicated lifecycles.

PHOTO FILE

Salmon leap upstream to reach their breeding grounds. Female salmon die just a few days after laying their eggs.

MY NOTES & PICTURES

I'VE SEEN A... Juvenile ◯ Adult ◯

SALMON *Salmo salar*

These fish are amongst the most interesting of British wildlife. They lead extraordinary lives that involve impressive migrations to the open sea and back again. They also feature in a famous autumn spectacle when they leap upstream to their spawning grounds. When water levels are high, these large fish hurl themselves up rivers and over weirs and waterfalls, before mating. Adults spend most of their lives at sea, eating squid, shrimp and small fish and they only return to freshwater to breed.

SCALE

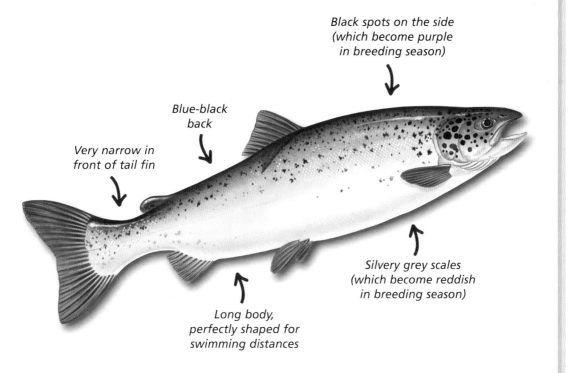

Black spots on the side
(which become purple
in breeding season)

Blue-black
back

Very narrow in
front of tail fin

Silvery grey scales
(which become reddish
in breeding season)

Long body,
perfectly shaped for
swimming distances

IN THE...   River ◯   Ocean ◯

FISH

FACT FILE

Size 4–6 cm

Habitat Freshwater and seawater

Found Widespread

Breeding Spawning occurs in spring and summer and the eggs are laid in a nest

SUPER FACT

Male sticklebacks build a nest and once the female has laid the eggs, he takes care of them. He fans the eggs with his fins to keep oxygen passing over them.

PHOTO FILE

A stickleback's large eyes contain special cells that can detect colour. They can probably see colours that are invisible to humans.

MY NOTES & PICTURES

I'VE SEEN A... Juvenile ◯ Adult ◯

THREE-SPINED STICKLEBACK

Gasterosteus aculeatus aculeatus

These sticklebacks are common in coastal areas or in freshwater, where there is plenty of vegetation to protect them from predators. They prefer places that have muddy or sandy bottoms. These fish usually live in large groups and feed on crustaceans, worms, insects, small fish, eggs and young fish (fry) of other species. At breeding time, male sticklebacks become very aggressive and may attack anything that is red, which they mistake for other males.

SCALE

MALE

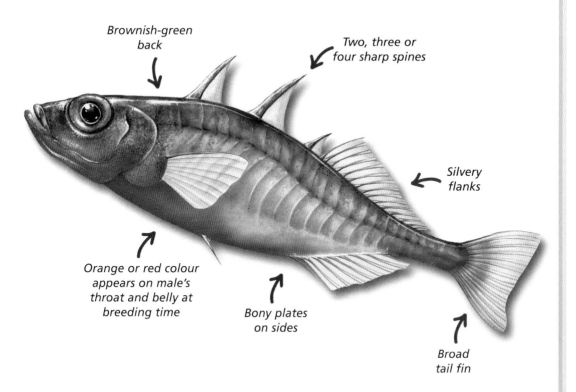

Brownish-green back

Two, three or four sharp spines

Silvery flanks

Orange or red colour appears on male's throat and belly at breeding time

Bony plates on sides

Broad tail fin

IN THE...   Freshwater ◯   Seawater ◯

BUGS

FACT FILE

Size 4–5 mm

Wings Males and queen ants

Habitat Underground, compost heaps

Breeding Queens lay thousands of eggs every month

SUPER FACT

Colonies in tropical regions can contain millions of ants. Some, such as driver and army ants, eat almost anything and can strip a tethered horse to its skeleton.

PHOTO FILE

Ants help plants to grow by breaking up the soil, and by carrying seeds and other food around the garden.

MY NOTES & PICTURES

I'VE SEEN A... Juvenile ◯ Adult ◯

ANT *Formicidae* family

Found in almost every habitat on land in the **world, ants live in large colonies.** They can be seen busily scurrying around a garden from spring to autumn, but are seen less often in winter when the temperatures are low. A colony of ants is divided into different types – the queen ant, female workers, and male ants. Some defend the nest, for example, while others are involved in reproduction.

ACTUAL SIZE

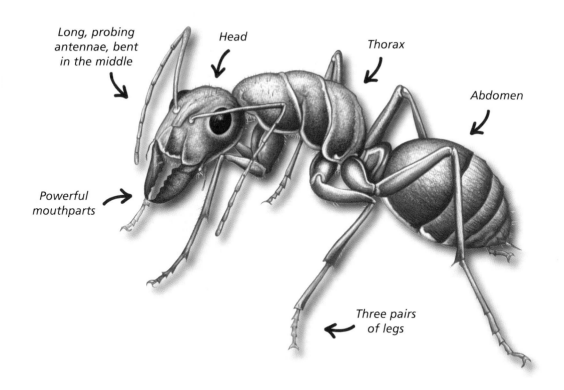

Long, probing antennae, bent in the middle

Head

Thorax

Abdomen

Powerful mouthparts

Three pairs of legs

IN THE... Garden Park Countryside

BUGS

FACT FILE

Size 1–3 cm

Wings Two pairs

Habitat Gardens, woodlands, parks

Breeding Queens lay more than 100 eggs a day

SUPER FACT

Bees communicate with each other in different ways, including 'dancing'. Honey bees returning to the hive use a dance to tell other bees where to find nectar.

PHOTO FILE

The bee's hairy body is covered with tiny specks of pollen. This yellow dust is part of a flower's reproductive system.

MY NOTES & PICTURES

I'VE SEEN A... Juvenile ◯   Adult ◯

BEE   *Apidae* family

One of the most important groups of insect, bees benefit both gardeners and farmers. They pollinate many plants, which is an essential part of fruit and seed production. Garden bumble bees, like honey bees, collect nectar from plants and feed pollen to their young. They are not aggressive insects and rarely sting. However, unlike honey bees, bumble bees can sting more than once. Some types of bumble bee are in danger of becoming extinct.

ACTUAL SIZE

FEMALE

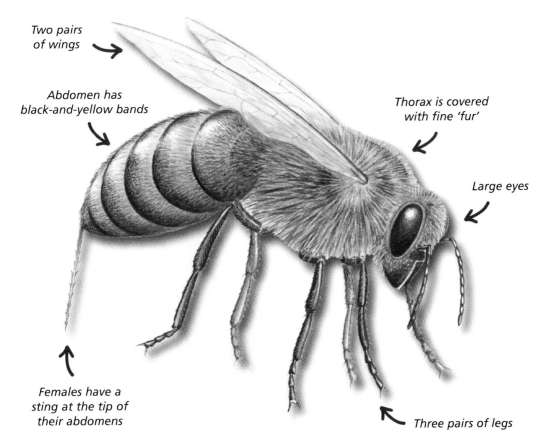

Two pairs of wings

Abdomen has black-and-yellow bands

Thorax is covered with fine 'fur'

Large eyes

Females have a sting at the tip of their abdomens

Three pairs of legs

IN THE... Garden   Park   Countryside

BUGS

FACT FILE

Size 1.2–2 cm

Wings None

Habitat Woodlands, farms, parks, heaths

Breeding Bluish-black larvae hatch in April, spend the summer eating, then mature into adults

SUPER FACT

These beetles get their name from their unusual form of defence. If attacked, they produce a red fluid from their mouth, which scares the predator and tastes bitter.

PHOTO FILE

The hard outer skin of a beetle is called an exoskeleton. It is made of a tough substance that is similar to that found in human nails.

MY NOTES & PICTURES

I'VE SEEN A... Juvenile ◯ Adult ◯

BLOODY-NOSED BEETLE *Timarcha tenebricosa*

Bloody-nosed beetles are widespread in **Britain, especially southern areas.** However, they are hard to spot because, like many other beetles, they are secretive animals. They can be found in hedgerows or other sheltered areas, and they are most active at night, although they can be seen scuttling around on hot summer days. These large beetles feed on the leaves of low-growing plants and hibernate until April, to avoid the cold winter months when food is in short supply.

ACTUAL SIZE

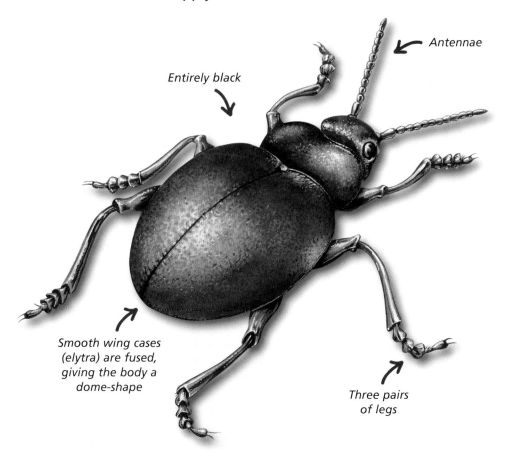

Antennae

Entirely black

Smooth wing cases (elytra) are fused, giving the body a dome-shape

Three pairs of legs

IN THE... Garden   Park   Countryside

BUGS

FACT FILE

Size Wingspan up to 6 cm

Wings Two pairs

Habitat Woodland and scrub

Breeding Eggs are laid in May, larvae pupate in June/July and adults emerge two weeks later

PHOTO FILE

The butterfly extends its long proboscis, which works like a bendy straw, into the flower and sucks up sugary nectar.

SUPER FACT

Butterflies may have been named after these yellow insects. Or perhaps from an ancient myth, which held that witches changed into butterflies to steal butter.

MY NOTES & PICTURES

I'VE SEEN A... Juvenile ◯   Adult ◯

BRIMSTONE BUTTERFLY *Gonepteryx rhamni*

Brimstone butterflies are widespread around Britain and other parts of Europe and North Africa. The caterpillars, which are bluish-green, feed on buckthorn and alder buckthorn leaves. The adults live on a diet of nectar, which they suck from flowers such as buddleia blooms. The adults emerge from their chrysalids in July and live until the following summer, following a winter hibernation. The females lay their eggs on the underside of buckthorn leaves, so the caterpillars emerge to a ready supply of food.

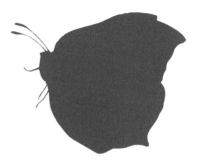

ACTUAL SIZE

MALE

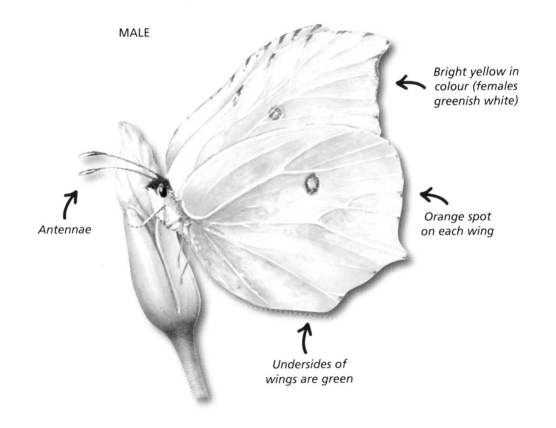

Bright yellow in colour (females greenish white)

Orange spot on each wing

Antennae

Undersides of wings are green

BUGS

FACT FILE

Size 1.8–2.2 cm

Wings None

Habitat Woods, hedges, gardens

Breeding Snails have male and female parts and can fertilize their own eggs

SUPER FACT

A cluster of empty snail shells next to a rock suggests that a thrush has been at work. These birds bash snails against a hard surface to break them.

PHOTO FILE

Like all snails, brown-lipped snails are molluscs, and belong to the same family as slugs, octopuses and shelled sea creatures.

MY NOTES & PICTURES

I'VE SEEN A... Juvenile ◯ Adult ◯

BROWN-LIPPED SNAIL *Cepaea nemoralis*

Brown-lipped snails are very similar to white-lipped snails, both in appearance and lifestyle. Their name indicates the best way to identify them; brown-lipped snails have a dark band on the rim of the shell. These molluscs are most active at night, when the ground is damp. They feed on grass and other low-growing plants, and are regarded by gardeners as destructive pests. Brown-lipped snails are also known as grove snails and are very common throughout Britain.

ACTUAL SIZE

Different banding patterns

Shell is brown, pale yellow or pinkish

Brown lip on margin of shell

Conical spire

Glossy, thin walls on shell

IN THE... Garden   Park   Countryside

189

BUGS

FACT FILE

Size 1.4–1.8 cm long
Wings Two pairs
Habitat Woodland
Breeding Larvae are yellowish-brown and live under bark

SUPER FACT

Black-headed cardinal beetles are most common in Wales and the Midlands, but the red-headed cardinal beetle is common throughout Britain.

PHOTO FILE

Adult red-headed cardinal beetles can be seen from May to July. They have thick, black comb-like antennae on their heads.

MY NOTES & PICTURES

I'VE SEEN A... Juvenile ◯   Adult ◯

CARDINAL BEETLE *Pyrochroa coccinea*

These beetles are very distinctive and easy to identify. Their bodies are long, flattened and bright red and their heads are either black or red. The hard outer casing on their bodies is formed of the forewings, which cover and protect the soft abdomen and second pair of wings underneath. Cardinal beetles fly from May to July and can sometimes be spotted on flowers or resting on tree trunks, particularly at the edges of woodlands.

ACTUAL SIZE

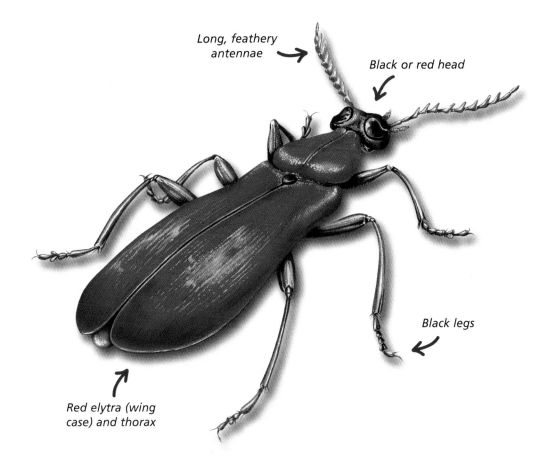

Long, feathery antennae

Black or red head

Black legs

Red elytra (wing case) and thorax

IN THE... Garden   Park   Countryside

BUGS

FACT FILE

Size 0.7–4 cm

Wings None

Habitat Leaf litter and soil

Breeding Larvae moult and grow many times

SUPER FACT

When young millipedes emerge from their eggs, they have short bodies and only three pairs of legs. They moult several times to allow their bodies, and legs, to grow.

PHOTO FILE

Snake millipedes have shiny, cylinder-shaped bodies. They live in leaf litter and climb trees and fences to feed at night.

MY NOTES & PICTURES

I'VE SEEN A... Juvenile ◯   Adult ◯

CENTIPEDE *Chilopoda superclass* and MILLIPEDE *Diplopoda superclass*

Those bugs aren't insects, and they belong to a group of creatures called myriapods. Centipedes and millipedes have long bodies that are divided into many segments. Centipedes have one pair of legs on each segment, while millipedes have two. The number of segments varies. The common centipede is chestnut brown in colour and adults have 15 pairs of legs. They hunt for insects, slugs and worms at night. Flat-backed millipedes live in compost heaps and leaf litter, and they eat plant matter.

ACTUAL SIZE

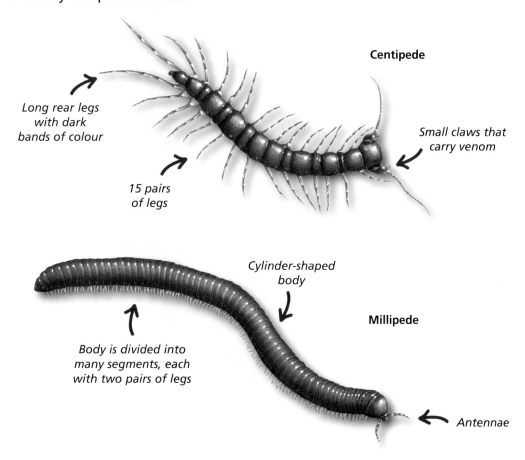

Centipede

Long rear legs with dark bands of colour

Small claws that carry venom

15 pairs of legs

Cylinder-shaped body

Millipede

Body is divided into many segments, each with two pairs of legs

Antennae

IN THE... Garden   Park   Countryside

FACT FILE

Size Up to 14 cm wingspan

Wings Two pairs

Habitat Farmland

Breeding The pale green caterpillars have purple and white stripes, and can grow up to 15 cm in length

SUPER FACT

These moths have the strange habit of crawling into beehives in search of honey. They can produce a loud squeaking noise if they are handled or startled.

PHOTO FILE

The death's head hawk moth is the largest moth in the UK. When it rests it holds its wings flat along its body, rather than upright.

MY NOTES & PICTURES

I'VE SEEN A... Juvenile ◯   Adult ◯

DEATH'S HEAD HAWK MOTH *Acherontia atropos*

This striking species of moth gets its name from the unusual pattern on the back of its thorax. This is the part of the body between the head and the fleshy abdomen. The pattern resembles a skull, which is also known as a 'death's head'. These moths are not native to Britain, but migrate, or travel, here for the summer. The larvae, or caterpillars, feed on potato plants, so the adults are more likely to be found in farms than in woods or gardens.

SCALE

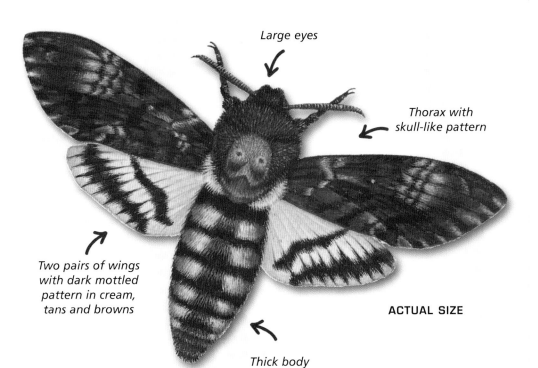

Large eyes

Thorax with skull-like pattern

Two pairs of wings with dark mottled pattern in cream, tans and browns

ACTUAL SIZE

Thick body

IN THE... Garden   Park   Countryside

BUGS

FACT FILE

Size 2–9 cm

Wings Two pairs

Habitat Near slow-moving or still water

Breeding Larvae are called nymphs

SUPER FACT

In ancient times, dragonflies were much bigger than they are today. Fossils of dragonflies show that their wingspans reached up to 75 cm!

PHOTO FILE

Dragonfly nymphs have large eyes and a thick body. Adults develop two pairs of wings and a longer, narrower abdomen.

MY NOTES & PICTURES

I'VE SEEN A... Juvenile ◯ Adult ◯

DRAGONFLY

Odonata order

Dragonflies are superb flyers and dart around in summer and autumn, visiting woodlands and gardens where there is water. They can be easily recognized by their long, slender bodies with colourful bands. Dragonflies have huge eyes that almost meet, and give them great vision. These insects spend most of their early lives underwater in ponds or lakes as nymphs. They can breathe underwater using their gills.

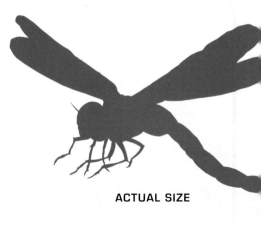

ACTUAL SIZE

MALE

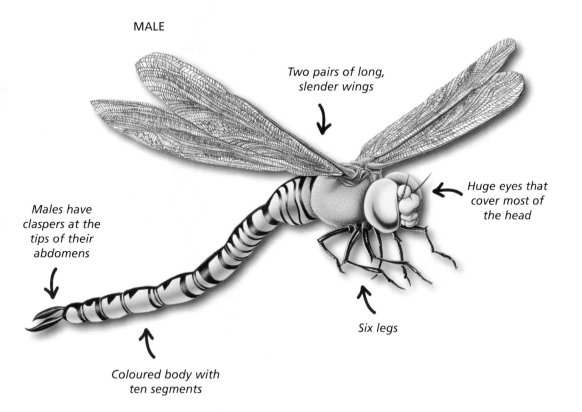

Two pairs of long, slender wings

Huge eyes that cover most of the head

Males have claspers at the tips of their abdomens

Coloured body with ten segments

Six legs

IN THE... Garden   Park   Countryside

BUGS

FACT FILE

Size Up to 9 mm

Wings Two pairs

Habitat Oak woodlands

Breeding Breed using galls,
or swellings, on trees that
protect the growing larvae

SUPER FACT

There are more than 1250 species
of gall wasp, many of them in
Europe and North America. Some
gall wasps are tiny, growing no
bigger than one mm.

PHOTO FILE

Some types of gall wasp look similar to ants.
Bees, ants and wasps belong to the same
group of insects, called Hymenoptera.

MY NOTES & PICTURES

I'VE SEEN A... Juvenile ◯ Adult ◯

GALL WASP *Cynips quercusfolii*

Gall wasps are not easy to find, but they
leave very interesting clues behind after
mating, which are simple to spot. These tiny
insects lay eggs inside plants, often on oak trees,
and by a process that remains a mystery, they
make the plant tissues grow and swell.
Eventually a gall is formed, which protects and
feeds the growing larvae inside. Different types
of gall wasp produce galls of different sizes and
shapes. They are related to wasps, bees and ants.

ACTUAL SIZE

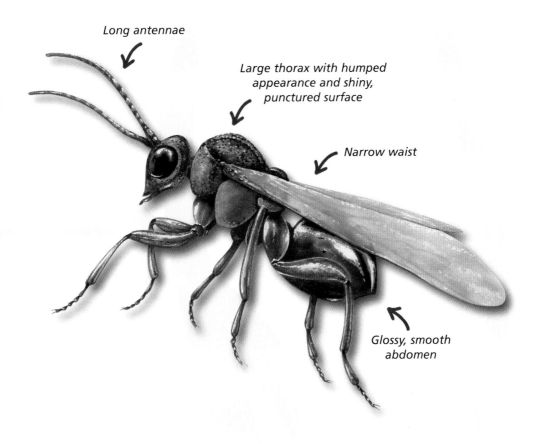

Long antennae

*Large thorax with humped
appearance and shiny,
punctured surface*

Narrow waist

*Glossy, smooth
abdomen*

IN THE... Garden   Park   Countryside

BUGS

FACT FILE

Size 1–1.4 cm (female)

Wings None

Habitat Gardens, parks, woodlands

Breeding Young are small, but fully-formed spiders

SUPER FACT

Spiders usually have eight eyes, eight legs, and are venomous. Their bodies are divided into two main segments – the cephalothorax and the abdomen.

PHOTO FILE

Garden spiders use silk to build their webs and capture their prey, such as flies. The fly will become wrapped in silk and then eaten.

MY NOTES & PICTURES

I'VE SEEN A... Juvenile ◯ Adult ◯

GARDEN SPIDER

Araneus diadematus

These spiders are usually brown, beige and
black in colour, although patterns do vary.
There are mottled white patches on the abdomen,
which often look like a cross. Females are about
twice the size of males. Garden spiders are common
in meadows, farms, woodlands and gardens. They
spin silk, which they use to build their webs and to
make cocoons to protect their eggs.

ACTUAL SIZE

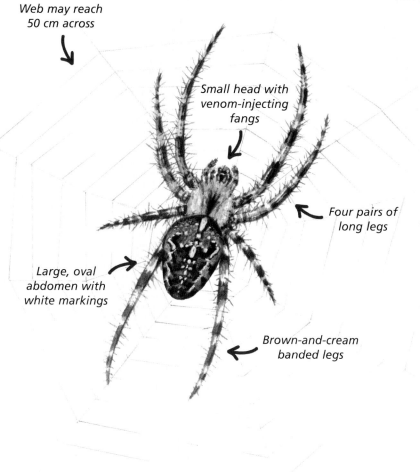

*Web may reach
50 cm across*

*Small head with
venom-injecting
fangs*

*Four pairs of
long legs*

*Large, oval
abdomen with
white markings*

*Brown-and-cream
banded legs*

IN THE... Garden   Park   Countryside

BUGS

FACT FILE

Size 2–2.5 cm (female)

Wings Two pairs

Habitat Grasslands, gardens, woodlands

Breeding Larvae are called nymphs

SUPER FACT

In some parts of the world grasshoppers are a popular food. Their legs and wings are removed before the body is fried in oil.

PHOTO FILE

Grasshoppers have large eyes and short antennae. Their mouthparts are adapted for eating grass and other tough plant materials.

MY NOTES & PICTURES

I'VE SEEN A... Juvenile ⭕   Adult ⭕

GRASSHOPPER *Orthoptera* order

With their large wings, grasshoppers **are good flyers, but usually prefer to escape from danger by leaping.** Usually green, they are well camouflaged against foliage. They have long, powerful legs that they use for jumping more than 20 times their own body length. Crickets have longer antennae than grasshoppers and can often be heard 'singing' on a summer's evening. The song sounds like a series of loud 'chirrups'.

ACTUAL SIZE

Tough forewings protect soft and delicate flying wings beneath

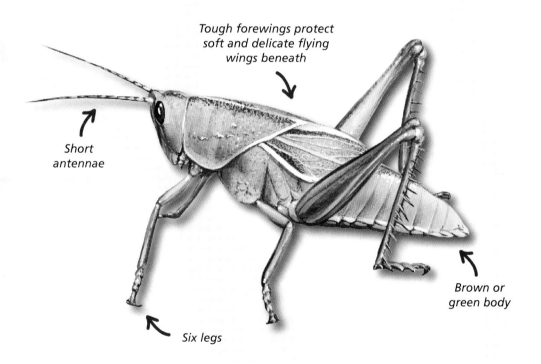

Short antennae

Brown or green body

Six legs

IN THE... Garden Park Countryside

BUGS

FACT FILE

Size 1–2.5 cm

Wings One pair

Habitat Woodland, rivers, marshes

Breeding Females lay up to 1000 eggs in a mass

SUPER FACT

Females use their enormous eyes to help them find their prey to bite. They can also detect carbon dioxide, the gas that humans and other animals breathe out.

PHOTO FILE

Like other insects, the horse fly's body is divided into three main parts. The thorax is the segment where a fly's wings are attached.

MY NOTES & PICTURES

I'VE SEEN A... Juvenile ◯　　　Adult ◯

HORSE FLY *Tabanidae* family

There are more than 4000 species of horse fly in the world and these are amongst the largest of all fly types. In Britain they are often found near wet habitats or around farms. The females bite humans or other animals and have razor-sharp mouthparts for cutting skin. They bite to get protein, which helps them produce bigger and healthier clusters of eggs. However, the males just suck nectar. The larvae are maggots. They live in mud and feed on rotting matter or small insects.

ACTUAL SIZE

FEMALE

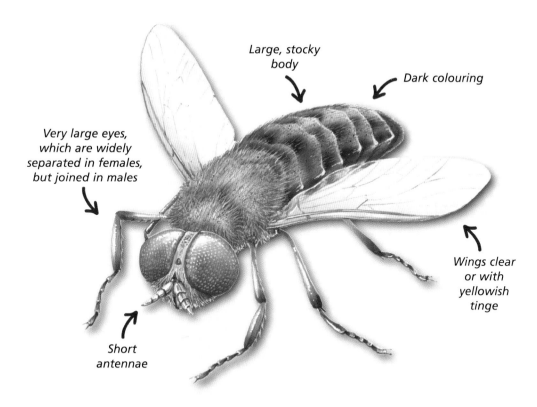

Large, stocky body

Dark colouring

Very large eyes, which are widely separated in females, but joined in males

Wings clear or with yellowish tinge

Short antennae

IN THE... Garden   Park   Countryside

BUGS

FACT FILE

Size Wingspan up to 5 cm

Wings Two pairs

Habitat Woodland, farms, gardens

Breeding Eggs are laid on long stalks to protect them from ants and other predators

SUPER FACT

Lacewings are equipped with sensors on their wings. These can detect ultrasound, which is a type of noise that is produced by bats when they are hunting insects.

PHOTO FILE

Adult lacewings hibernate in the winter and often come into houses in the autumn, looking for somewhere safe to rest.

MY NOTES & PICTURES

I'VE SEEN A... Juvenile ◯   Adult ◯

LACEWING *Chrysopidae* family

Green lacewings have slender, delicate bodies and long flimsy wings that are veined and almost transparent. There are more than 1600 species of lacewing and most of them are only active at night. They are predators and attack all sorts of other insects, especially those with soft bodies, such as caterpillars and aphids. For this reason, they are often bred in large numbers and released on farmland to reduce the number of pests, without the need for chemical pesticides.

ACTUAL SIZE

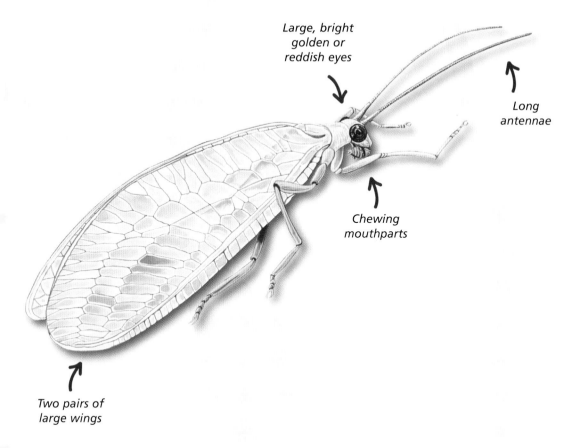

Large, bright golden or reddish eyes

Long antennae

Chewing mouthparts

Two pairs of large wings

IN THE... Garden   Park   Countryside

BUGS

FACT FILE

Size 5–8 mm

Wings Two pairs

Habitat Gardens, woodlands

Breeding Blue larvae with cream spots

SUPER FACT

When handled, ladybirds produce drops of smelly yellow fluid from their legs to deter predators from eating them. Their bright colours warn predators to stay away.

PHOTO FILE

The seven-spot ladybird has three spots on each elytron. The seventh spot is where the elytra, which protect the wings, meet.

MY NOTES & PICTURES

I'VE SEEN A... Juvenile ◯ Adult ◯

LADYBIRD   *Coccinella 7-punctata*

Brightly coloured beetles, ladybirds have round bodies and hard wing cases, called elytra. Adults spend winter in large groups, hidden under loose bark on trees or crammed into crevices. Ladybird larvae hatch from small eggs that are glued to plants either singly or in small groups. They mostly eat other soft-bodied animals. Adult ladybirds are important predators of aphids, making them especially welcome in gardens. Thirteen-spot and five-spot ladybirds are very rare and seldom seen in the UK. The two-spot ladybird is smaller than its seven-spotted cousin and their colours vary from region to region.

ACTUAL SIZE

Antennae are used to detect smells

Hard outer wings (elytra) protect soft, flying wings underneath

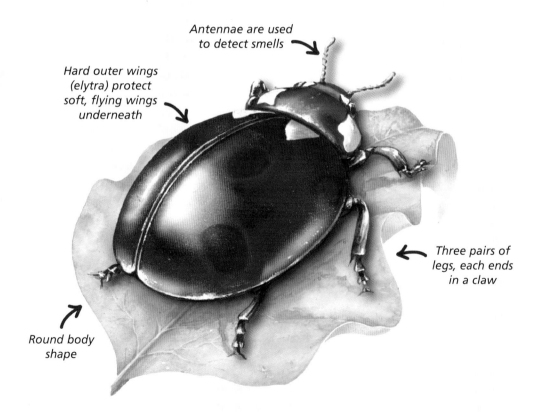

Three pairs of legs, each ends in a claw

Round body shape

IN THE...   Garden   Park   Countryside

BUGS

FACT FILE

Size Up to 1.5 cm
Wings Two pairs
Habitat Ponds, canals
Breeding Eggs are laid in spring
and are attached to plants

SUPER FACT

Both types of swimming water
boatmen may appear silvery. This
is due to a large air bubble that
the insects carry with them so
they can breathe underwater.

PHOTO FILE

A water boatman, or common backswimmer,
swims upside down and moves itself forward
using its long hind limbs like oars.

MY NOTES & PICTURES

I'VE SEEN A... Juvenile ◯   Adult ◯

LESSER WATER BOATMAN *Corixa punctata*

These beetles swim in ponds and eat plant matter, often scraping algae off rocks or other surfaces. They use their unusually long legs like paddles as they move swiftly through the water. They are preyed upon by animals such as dragonfly larvae and birds. Although lesser water boatmen look similar to water boatmen, or common backswimmers, they actually belong to a different group of beetles. Lesser water boatmen swim on their fronts, while water boatmen swim on their backs and are predators, hunting tadpoles, small fish and flying insects that fall in the water.

ACTUAL SIZE

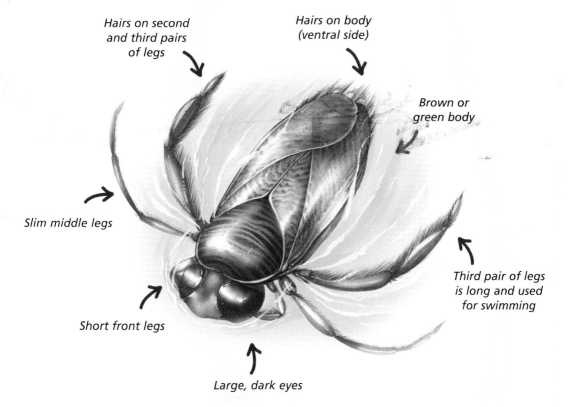

Hairs on second and third pairs of legs

Hairs on body (ventral side)

Brown or green body

Slim middle legs

Third pair of legs is long and used for swimming

Short front legs

Large, dark eyes

IN THE... **Pond** **Canal**

BUGS

FACT FILE

Size 2 cm

Wings Two pairs

Habitat Ponds, still waters

Breeding Males and females mate on the surface of the water and the female lays her eggs on land

SUPER FACT

Pond skaters avoid freezing to death on ice-covered water by hibernating in the winter. They fly long distances to find a safe resting place until April.

PHOTO FILE

A pond skater uses its hind legs to steer, its middle legs to push itself forward and its front legs to capture prey.

MY NOTES & PICTURES

I'VE SEEN A... Juvenile ◯　　　　Adult ◯

POND SKATER *Gerris lacustris*

Pond skaters are fascinating creatures to watch as they speed across the surface of the water, without breaking its surface. These bugs are also known as waterstriders and they are widespread throughout Britain. Pond skaters can detect prey by sensing the vibrations on the water surface caused when an insect falls into the water. Within seconds, the pond skater has located its prey and grabs it with its short, stout front legs. If attacked themselves, pond skaters can jump out of danger.

ACTUAL SIZE

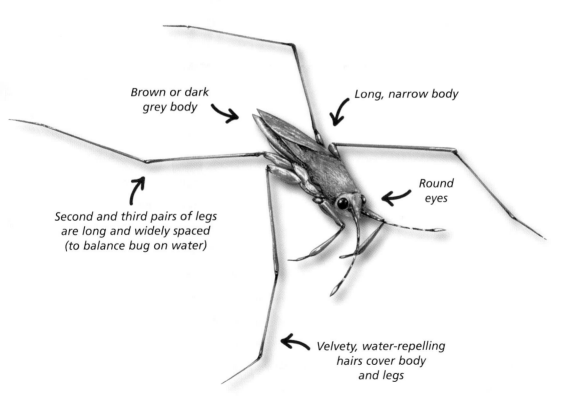

Brown or dark grey body

Long, narrow body

Second and third pairs of legs are long and widely spaced (to balance bug on water)

Round eyes

Velvety, water-repelling hairs cover body and legs

IN THE...   Pond   Lake

BUGS

FACT FILE

Size Wingspan up to 6 cm

Wings Two pairs

Habitat Gardens, meadows

Breeding Eggs are laid singularly on nettle leaves

SUPER FACT

The larvae of red admirals (caterpillars) are normally dark and bristled, but the colour varies from green–grey–black with yellow lines on either side.

PHOTO FILE

Butterflies use their straw-like mouthpart, the proboscis, to suck nectar from flowers, such as buddleia, or feed on rotting fruit.

MY NOTES & PICTURES

I'VE SEEN A... Juvenile ◯   Adult ◯

RED ADMIRAL BUTTERFLY *Vanessa atalanta*

Named after their 'admirable' colours, these butterflies are easily recognized by their dark-coloured wings with red bands and white spots. They have hints of blue and black spots on their hind wings. Red admirals are fast, powerful flyers and – unusually for butterflies – may fly at night. These insects are found throughout the UK and Europe and inhabit gardens, parks, woodlands, seashores and mountains.

ACTUAL SIZE

Red bands on forewings

Long antennae used for smelling and touching

Red patches along the back of hind wings

Edges of wings lined with blue spots

IN THE... Garden   Park   Countryside

BUGS

FACT FILE

Size 4–5.5 cm wingspan

Wings Two pairs

Habitat Flowery gardens, meadows

Breeding Heaps of eggs are laid on the underside of nettle leaves in April

SUPER FACT

Its Latin name, *Aglais urticae*, comes from the word for nettles, *urtica*, because this is the butterfly's favourite food.

PHOTO FILE

These insects rest with their wings closed, but flap them to alarm predators with their bright colours.

MY NOTES & PICTURES

I'VE SEEN A... Juvenile ◯ Adult ◯

SMALL TORTOISESHELL BUTTERFLY *Aglais urticae*

Named after their colouring, small tortoiseshells are often one of the first types of butterfly to be seen in spring. Adults emerge from hibernation in March or April and mate soon afterwards. They lay their eggs on food plants, such as nettles, and they hatch about ten days later. Small tortoiseshells are common butterflies and live in a range of habitats, particularly near human homes. They spend winter in sheds, garages and gardens.

ACTUAL SIZE

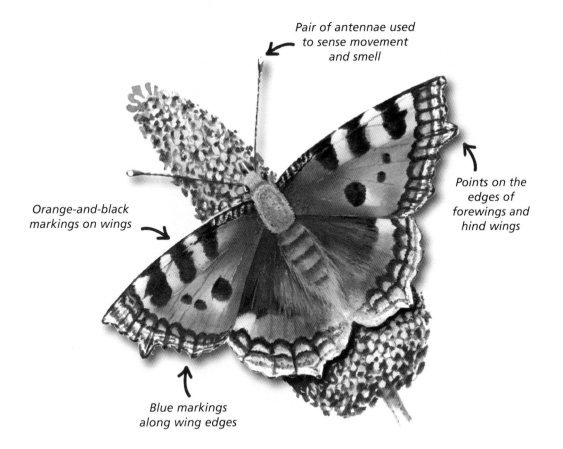

Pair of antennae used to sense movement and smell

Points on the edges of forewings and hind wings

Orange-and-black markings on wings

Blue markings along wing edges

IN THE... Garden   Park   Countryside

BUGS

FACT FILE

Size 2–8 cm

Wings Two pairs

Habitat Woodlands, gardens

Breeding White larvae with brown heads

SUPER FACT

Stag beetles were common in gardens and parklands, but they have become increasingly rare over the last 50 years and are now threatened with extinction.

PHOTO FILE

Eggs are laid in rotting wood. Larvae feed on wood for up to six years before they pupate. Adults emerge in summer.

MY NOTES & PICTURES

I'VE SEEN A... Juvenile ◯   Adult ◯

STAG BEETLE *Lucanus cervus*

One of the largest and most impressive insects, **stag beetles can be heard as they noisily fly at dusk, searching for mates.** Adults may only live for a few months and can survive without feeding. Males have large mouthparts, called mandibles, which they use to fight one another for females. Gardens with undisturbed areas of rotting wood may attract these endangered animals, as the larvae feed on wood.

ACTUAL SIZE

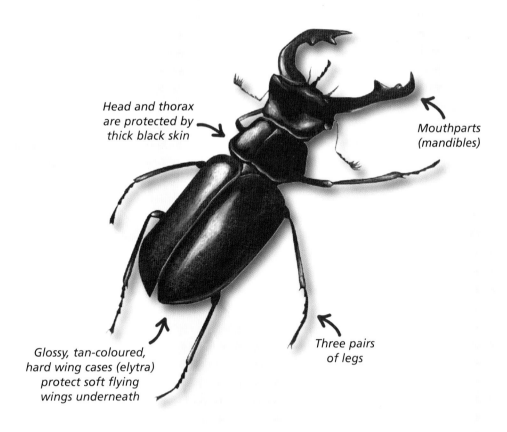

Head and thorax are protected by thick black skin

Mouthparts (mandibles)

Glossy, tan-coloured, hard wing cases (elytra) protect soft flying wings underneath

Three pairs of legs

IN THE... Garden   Park   Countryside

BUGS

FACT FILE

Size Up to 8 cm wingspan

Wings Two pairs

Habitat Marshland

Breeding Eggs are laid in several broods from April–September and they may hatch the same year, or the next

SUPER FACT

Swallowtails used to be common in many British marshlands, but they are now found only in the marshes around the Norfolk Broads.

PHOTO FILE

Unlike most butterflies, swallowtails also eat pollen. The extra protein in pollen helps them to live longer than most types of butterfly.

MY NOTES & PICTURES

I'VE SEEN A... Juvenile ◯ Adult ◯

SWALLOWTAIL BUTTERFLY *Papilio machaon*

Swallowtails are Britain's largest butterflies **and amongst the most attractive.** Their names describe the long 'tails' that grow at the back of the hindwings. The larvae start their lives as black-and-white caterpillars that resemble bird droppings, which protects them from predators. As they grow they turn green and black, with orange marks, and produce a foul smell to keep predators at bay. The adults feed on nectar and the larvae feed only on milk parsley.

SCALE

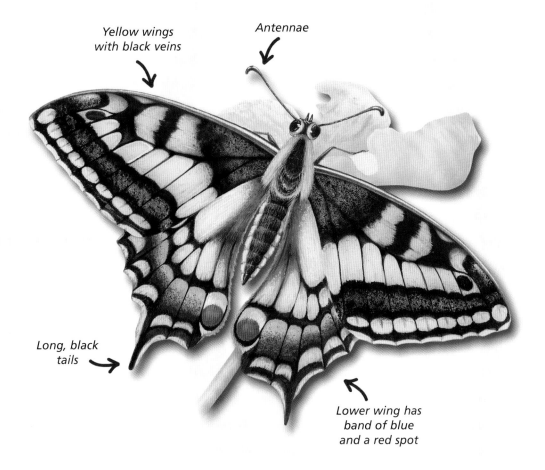

Yellow wings with black veins

Antennae

Long, black tails

Lower wing has band of blue and a red spot

IN THE... Garden   Park   Countryside

BUGS

FACT FILE

Size 0.4–1.5 cm

Wings None

Habitat Grasslands, gardens, coasts

Breeding After mating with a female, the male has to escape her clutches, or risk being eaten

SUPER FACT

Wasp spiders live in southern areas, as they actually come from Mediterranean countries.
If global warming continues, they may move further north.

PHOTO FILE

This wasp spider is carefully wrapping its prey in layers of silk, which it has produced in its body. The spider will devour the prey later.

MY NOTES & PICTURES

I'VE SEEN A... Juvenile ◯ Adult ◯

WASP SPIDER *Argiope bruennichi*

The distinctive wasp spider is easy to identify, with its bold pattern of stripes. This banding may deter predators, such as birds, which think the stripes signify a sting or poison. However, it is only seen on females, which are more colourful than the dull males, and much bigger too. Wasp spiders prey on flying insects and grasshoppers, which they catch in their orb webs. They wrap their captured prey in silk before devouring them.

ACTUAL SIZE

Abdomen is covered with yellow, black and white horizontal stripes, but males are pale brown

Large abdomen is oval in shape

FEMALE

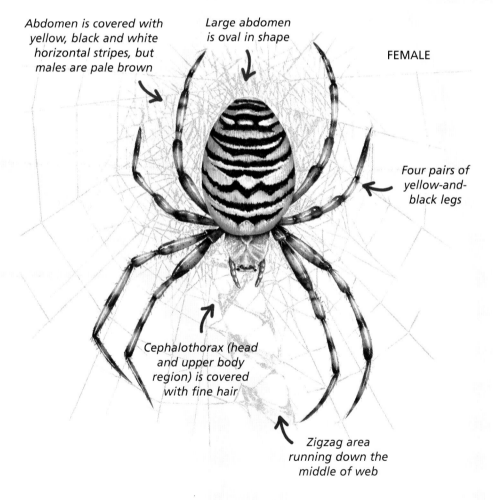

Four pairs of yellow-and-black legs

Cephalothorax (head and upper body region) is covered with fine hair

Zigzag area running down the middle of web

IN THE... Garden   Park   Countryside

GLOSSARY

Abdomen The rear part of an insect's body, which usually appears segmented.

Antennae A pair of long, sensitive feelers on an insect's head.

Carnivore An animal that feeds on meat.

Colony A large number of animals that live together in an organized group.

Elytra The hard outer wings of a beetle.

Habitat An animal's or plant's natural home.

Herbivore An animal that feeds on plants.

Hibernate To spend the winter in a deep sleep.

Juvenile A young animal.

Larvae Insects that have emerged from their eggs but have not yet become adults (for example, caterpillars).

Nocturnal Animals that are active at night.

Predator An animal that hunts, catches and kills other animals (their prey).

Prey Any animal that is hunted and then eaten by other animals.

Territory An area that an animal treats as its own and defends against others.

Thorax The middle section of an insect's body, where the wings (if there are any) and legs are attached.

Acknowledgements

The publishers would like to thank the following artists who have contributed to this book:

Ian Jackson, Mike Saunders

All other artworks from the Miles Kelly Artwork Bank

The publishers would like to thank the following sources for the use of their photographs:

Cover: Rechitan Sorin/Shutterstock

1 Menno Schaefer/Shutterstock; 3 Herbert Kratky/Fotolia; 6(t) Van Truan/Fotolia, (bl) Canon_Bob/Fotolia; 7(t) Gunta Klavina/Fotolia; 8(tl) Brian Lambert/Fotolia, (tr) B. Borrell Casals/FLPA; 11(t) Jeremy Turner/Fotolia, (bl) Dave Timms/Fotolia; 14(t) John Barber/Fotolia, (bl) Robert Ford/Fotolia; 15(b) Jp Nel/Fotolia; 16(m) Steve Mutch/Fotolia; 17(m) Victor Vecteur/Fotolia, (bl) Frédéric Chausse/Fotolia; 18(r) Iouri Timofeev/Fotolia; 19(t) AndreasG/Fotolia, (b) Gail Johnson/Fotolia; 20(t) Anneke Schram/Fotolia; 21(b) Michel Gatti/Fotolia; 24 Luc Patureau/Fotolia; 30 Hugh Clark/FLPA; 32 Derek Middleton/FLPA; 34 Derek A Robinson/FLPA; 36 David Hoskins/FLPA; 38 Wil Meinderts/Foto Natura/FLPA; 40 Hugo Willocx/Foto Natura/FLPA; 42 Roger Hosking/FLPA; 44 Colin Varndell; 46 marilyna/Fotolia; 48 Gregory Smellinckx/Fotolia; 50 Paul Hobson/FLPA; 52 Eiena Biokhina/Fotolia; 54 Phil McLean/FLPA; 56 Roger Tidman/FLPA; 58 Derek Middleton/FLPA; 62 Jan Vermeer/Foto Natura/FLPA; 64 B. Borrell Casals/FLPA; 66 Silvestris Fotoservice/FLPA; 68 Derek Middleton/FLPA; 70 Nigel Cattlin/FLPA; 72 Cyril Ruoso/JH Editorial/Minden Pictures/FLPA; 78 Hans Dieter Brand/FLPA; 80 Peter Bialas/Fotolia; 82 Derek Middleton/FLPA; 84 Mike Lane/FLPA; 86 Ronnie Howard/Fotolia; 88 Jurgen & Christine Sohns/FLPA; 90 Panda Photo/FLPA; 98 Wil Meinderts/Foto Natura/FLPA; 102 Roger Tidman/FLPA; 106 John Hawkins/FLPA; 118 jltfoto/Fotolia; 124 ril/Fotolia; 126 Paul Hobson/FLPA; 128 Christophe Fouquin/Fotolia; 132 Phil McLean/FLPA; 134 Gail Johnson/Fotolia; 136 Roger Wilmshurst/FLPA; 138 Christian Marx/Fotolia; 140 Paul Hobson/FLPA; 144 Konrad Wothe/Minden Pictures/FLPA; 146 Roger Wilmhurst/FLPA; 150 Roger Tidman/FLPA; 154 Paul Murphy/Fotolia; 156 Shane Kennedy/Fotolia; 160 Tony Hamblin/FLPA; 162 Mike Lane/FLPA; 164 Derek Middleton/FLPA; 166 Walter Rohdich/FLPA; 168 Norbert Wu/Minden Pictures/FLPA; 170 Wendy Dennis/FLPA; 172 Reinhard Ditscher/FLPA; 174 Wil Meinderts/Foto Natura/FLPA; 176 Sunset/FLPA; 178 Silvestris Fotoservice/FLPA; 180 Ismael Montero/Fotolia; 188 Malcolm Schuyl/FLPA; 190 Drac/Fotolia; 192 Bine/Fotolia; 194 Ingo Arndt/Foto Natura/Minden Pictures/FLPA; 196 Derek Middleton/FLPA; 198 Mark Moffett/Minden Pictures/FLPA; 200 Heidi & Hans-Jurgen Koch/Minden Pictures/FLPA; 204 Martin B Withers/FLPA; 208 Martina Moser/Fotolia; 210 Derek Middleton/FLPA; 212 Colin Varndell; 214 criber/Fotolia; 216 Andy Mac/Fotolia; 218 AZ-/Fotolia; 220 Paul Cowan/Fotolia

All other photographs from:
digitalSTOCK, digitalvision, Dreamstime.com, Fotolia.com, iStockphoto.com, John Foxx, PhotoAlto, PhotoDisc, PhotoEssentials, PhotoPro, Stockbyte, WTPL